Praise for
The *Kindness* Challenge

"Some sociologists have called our culture the argument culture. We focus on our differences and freely shoot verbal bombs at each other. I can't believe that any of us are happy with the divisiveness we have created. Is there a road back to civility? I believe there is, and Shaunti Feldhahn is pointing the way with *The Kindness Challenge*. I highly recommend this book and believe it has the potential to change the emotional climate of our culture."

—GARY CHAPMAN, *New York Times* best-selling author
of *The Five Love Languages*

"This book is an amazingly powerful tool that will transform your heart and your relationships from the inside out."

—LYSA TERKEURST, *New York Times* best-selling author
and president of Proverbs 31 Ministries

"Shaunti Feldhahn did it again. Where others make guesses, she does research. Kindness isn't just something nice to do; it's a game changer in all of our relationships. I encourage you to take that kindness challenge."

—CHIP INGRAM, founder of Living on the Edge and senior pastor
of Venture Christian Church

"If kindness means care and concern for others, when would it ever be the wrong approach? Imagine a world that is not rude, self-serving, impatient, and hurried. Shaunti Feldhahn challenges us to rise above culture, open our hearts, and experience the life changing benefits of kindness. We desperately need this kindness challenge!"

—CHERYL A. BACHELDER, CEO of Popeyes Louisiana Kitchen Inc.
and author of *Dare to Serve*

"Just when I thought I understood what it meant to be kind, along came Shaunti Feldhahn. Her compelling evidence taught me that there's more than meets the eye when it comes to weaving kindness into our everyday lives. After reading this book, I took the challenge—and it transformed my relationships. Shaunti believes kindness is a superpower, and I agree 100 percent."

—CHRIS BROWN, national radio show host of *Chris Brown's True Stewardship,* a division of Dave Ramsey Solutions

"In her latest book, Shaunti Feldhahn has touched on one of the most important elements of any healthy relationship—kindness! We all know we should be kind, but do we know why? And *how*? Shaunti has provided an inspiring road-map for anyone who wants to nurture their most important relationships."

—JIM DALY, president of Focus on the Family

"This concept is so simple, so profound, so doable, and so inspiring. I am taking the kindness challenge, and it is making a difference in my heart and in my home. Truly, as Shaunti's research proves, the kinder you are, the happier you are. I am recommending this book to everyone who has any relationship issues or anyone who just flat-out wants to be a happier, wiser person."

—JENNIFER ROTHSCHILD, author of *Lessons I Learned in the Dark* and *Me, Myself, and Lies*

"Struggling to show kindness to that difficult person in your life? This book will equip you with the motivation, the inspiration, and the practical tools to transform your relationships—even for those really hard-to-love co-workers and family members!"

—CRYSTAL PAINE, founder of MoneySavingMom.com and *New York Times* best-selling author of *Say Goodbye to Survival Mode*

"I hope *The Kindness Challenge* becomes a worldwide movement of changed lives. The power of kindness has the capacity to transform any marriage, family, and even work environment. You can't take on this challenge and not improve your life. I took Shaunti's kindness challenge personally, and I invite you to do the same. Kindness matters. Spread the word."

—JIM BURNS, PhD, president of HomeWord, author of *Creating an Intimate Marriage* and *Confident Parenting*

"Shaunti Feldhahn is the Relationship Whisperer. Her groundbreaking research, brilliant insights, practical applications, and inspiring calls to action will transform your relationships in profound ways. Imagine how different your life would look if your most difficult relationship became one of your healthiest. *The Kindness Challenge* can make that a reality. Shaunti lays out a compelling plan that has already improved countless relationships, and it will undoubtedly work for you as well. Guaranteed."

—DAVE AND ASHLEY WILLIS, best-selling authors and founders
of StrongerMarriages.org

"*The Kindness Challenge* is the right book at the right time. With our world becoming harsher and coarser, Shaunti's message of love is a God-sent antidote. She's captured how being kind changes our hearts toward other people, and how God mysteriously uses that kindness superpower to change everything! Get ready to be rocked by kindness."

—CHUCK FINNEY, president of Finney Media

"Got a grumpy neighbor? A rocky relationship with a friend? A family member who gets on your very last nerve? If you've ever longed to see these people change their behavior, then this book . . . well, it won't do that. But it *will* empower you to change the four things you actually can: your perspective, your attitude, your actions, and your reactions. *The Kindness Challenge* is a practical tool that will transform the way you view—and treat—others as you make it your habit to praise rather than pester, to impart kindness rather than criticism, and to treat others with generosity and dignity, just as Jesus did. Highly recommended!"

—KAREN EHMAN, Proverbs 31 Ministries speaker and *New York
Times* best-selling author of *Keep It Shut* and *Listen, Love, Repeat*

"Shaunti has done it again! *The Kindness Challenge* is another example of how she pulls golden nuggets out of research. She offers up three easy, practical steps you can make in your relationships to take them to the next level."

—CRAIG GROSS, founder of XXXchurch.com and co-author
of *Through a Man's Eyes*

"Stop whatever you're doing and read this book! Take the challenge! Why? Because it's about to revolutionize your relationships. All of them. And it's easier than you might imagine. Shaunti lays out a proven and practical plan that anyone can follow. Your life won't be the same after reading this book."

—DRS. LES AND LESLIE PARROTT, #1 *New York Times* best-selling authors of *Saving Your Marriage Before It Starts*

"We are all looking for the easy button in relationships. Shaunti has helped us find it. While it's not always easy to be kind—especially when we really don't want to be—it matters greatly in the relationships that mean so much to us. I'm taking the words on these pages seriously, and I hope you will too!"

—JILL SAVAGE, CEO of Hearts at Home and author of *No More Perfect Marriages*

"Shaunti Feldhahn is right when she says kindness is a superpower. Whether you decide to embrace the kindness challenge for your spouse, child, or neighbor, your life will be changed. *The Kindness Challenge* is a great first step in loving others well."

—MARK AND SUSAN MERRILL, founders of Family First, All Pro Dad, and iMom

"In a world that understands payback but not patience, a world that is not only thoughtless but has completely forgotten how to say thank you, *The Kindness Challenge* is a desperately needed resource. Learning not only to get along with people but to invest in them with the purposeful, intentional act of being kind is both world changing and people changing. Take the challenge to change those you love with kindness—and let kindness change the very essence of who you are."

—KATHI LIPP, best-selling author of *The Husband Project, Clutter Free,* and *Overwhelmed*

THE Kindness CHALLENGE

Thirty Days to Improve Any Relationship

SHAUNTI FELDHAHN

WATERBROOK

The Kindness Challenge

Details in some anecdotes and stories have been changed to protect the identities of the persons involved.

Trade Paperback ISBN 978-1-60142-122-7
eBook ISBN 978-1-60142-359-7

Jacket design by Lucy Iloenyosi, NeatWorks Inc.

Published in association with the literary agency of Calvin W. Edwards, 1220 Austin Glen Drive, Atlanta, Georgia 30338.

Published in the United States by WaterBrook, an imprint of the Crown Publishing Group, a division of Penguin Random House LLC, New York.

WATERBROOK® and its deer colophon are registered trademarks of Penguin Random House LLC.

Library of Congress Cataloging-in-Publication Data
Names: Feldhahn, Shaunti, author.
Title: The kindness challenge : thirty days to improve any relationship / Shaunti Feldhahn.
Description: Colorado Springs, Colorado : WaterBrook, 2016. | "First Edition." | Includes bibliographical references.
Identifiers: LCCN 2016032574 (print) | LCCN 2016039685 (ebook) | ISBN 9781601421227 (hard cover) | ISBN 9781601423597 (electronic)
Subjects: LCSH: Kindness. | Interpersonal relations.
Classification: LCC BJ1533.K5 F45 2016 (print) | LCC BJ1533.K5 (ebook) | DDC 158.2—dc23
LC record available at https://lccn.loc.gov/2016032574

Printed in the United States of America
2016—First Edition

10 9 8 7 6 5 4 3 2 1

SPECIAL SALES
Most WaterBrook books are available at special quantity discounts when purchased in bulk by corporations, organizations, and special-interest groups. Custom imprinting or excerpting can also be done to fit special needs. For information, please e-mail specialmarketscms@penguinrandom house.com or call 1-800-603-7051.

To all those who choose kindness.

Be kind, for everyone you meet is fighting a great battle.

—PHILO OF ALEXANDRIA

Contents

Matters

've seen a remarkable pattern during a decade of surveying thousands of people about their inner insecurities and needs—a pattern that upends all our ideas about what leads us to thrive in life.

I've seen what makes us miserable and what lights us up, and as you might guess, it makes a big difference when our needs are being met and when others know how to avoid hurting us. It makes a big difference when we experience fulfillment at work, and love and appreciation at home.

But above all that is one greater factor: *whether we thrive depends far more on how we choose to treat others than on how we ourselves are treated.* In fact, when handled well, that one factor often leads to those other things that light us up. When handled poorly, it often leads to misery.

The path to our happy place starts with one choice: whether or not to be kind. Especially when we really don't want to be.

In the pages ahead, we'll tackle the surprising truth of what kindness (or unkindness) really means in practice and how easy it is to be unkind without ever realizing it. You'll see how kindness can transform your home, romantic partnership, parenting, leadership, school, workplace, church, sports, community, governance, job. . . . Our kindness matters in so many places, and it is where and when we least want to give it that it has the greatest power to transform.

We'll explore how much kindness matters in our personal and professional relationships. Do you want to get along well with people and help others do the same? Most of us do. Is there a specific someone with whom you want or need a better relationship? Most of us have that too.

It turns out the seemingly gentle quality of kindness has an explosive power, but we don't always know how to unleash it. What are the specific, simple steps that make the difference? Why do certain actions matter so much and work so well—in any type of relationship or for our whole culture? How can you apply them so you become a person whose life is marked by kindness and so you and those around you thrive?

I'll be sharing the what, why, and how of the most practical and strategic answers in the chapters ahead, including a specific how-to plan that we call the 30-Day Kindness Challenge. I've seen this Challenge transform thousands of relationships: those between spouses, colleagues, families, and business and social partnerships. But better still, it also transforms us.

THE LIFE-CHANGING POWER OF KINDNESS

If you're like the majority of those we've surveyed over the years, a few things are true. Most of your people problems don't stem from the big systemic issues but from the little ones. You don't like living with difficulty and strain in your personal life, in your workplace, or in society at large. You are willing to show more graciousness, kindness, and generosity to have better relationships. But you're busy, stretched, and frustrated, and you may think some little act won't matter. Or you've tried everything you can think of, and those things haven't worked. Perhaps you don't know how or where to start, so the end result is the same: you're living with a contentious situation that is reducing your enjoyment of life.

Yet in most cases, it doesn't have to be that way.

The research is clear: so many of our everyday relationships today don't need to be hurtful or difficult. Once your eyes are open to this, you'll see two types of kindness that have great power to transform:

1. Targeted kindness that is specific to one individual—for example, a spouse, boyfriend, girlfriend, child, classmate, or colleague— with whom you want a better relationship.

2. Broad kindness that impacts the many people you encounter and thus the culture at large.

Although we're focusing primarily on targeted kindness in this book, all the principles can be adapted broadly for society.

It turns out that kindness is made up of three distinct elements: areas of *thought, word,* and *action* we may never have connected with kindness before. As we investigate these, most of us will discover dozens of ways we have been *un*kind and never realized it—ways we have been sabotaging ourselves and our personal relationships, workplace effectiveness, activities, and enjoyment of life. Becoming aware of this "kindness blindness" is a surprisingly powerful outcome all by itself, but we'll also discover kindness strengths that we did not know mattered and upon which we can build.

This book will help us figure out which specific elements of kindness we need to work on and how, identify specific actions we might need to do (or not do!), and then dare each of us to take the 30-Day Kindness Challenge, not just to improve a specific relationship but to be part of a culture-transforming movement. And once we put these elements into practice, that's when our eyes will be opened to what truly matters most—both for our lives and for those relationships that are most important to us.

Here's what this will look like.

ROAD MAP FOR THE JOURNEY AHEAD

Part 1 of the book shows why kindness, above all other character traits, is particularly important for thriving in life, work, and relationships, and yet why we are so easily deluded about how kind or unkind we actually are.

Part 2 unpacks the three elements of kindness and the 30-Day Kindness Challenge so each of us can identify our own individual patterns of kindness (or the lack of it) that we may never have noticed before.

Finally, in Part 3 you'll find specific tools to help put kindness into practice in the form of daily tips for whatever version of the 30-Day Kindness Challenge you choose to do. (You can also sign up for daily e-mail reminders and personal assessments at JoinTheKindnessChallenge.com—including a printable Self-Assessment Action Plan for before and after the Challenge—find links to social media tools, and get resources for doing the Challenge with others or with your organization.)

To get the most out of this process, I suggest that you read the book with a pen and journal or notebook within reach. Circle or jot notes about those things that apply to your life and to the person (or people) with whom you want a better relationship. Capture what you most need to tackle. Then, when you actually do the 30-Day Kindness Challenge, you can track your learning and progress, as well as how the other person responds, and get advice from others. As you continue to apply that learning, you will improve how you approach that person, make adjustments, track his or her reactions to those adjustments, and so on. Soon you will have walked yourself along the road to life-altering transformation in that relationship—and in our culture.

Want to take the Challenge? Let's get started.

Part I

Why a Little
Kindness
Makes a Big Difference

Kindness Makes the World Go Round

The Surprising Importance of a Simple Challenge

On a winter day ten years ago in Colorado, I was speaking at a women's conference, sharing some research about men from my newly released book, *For Women Only*. I explained the surprising discovery that men doubt themselves far more than women realize and thus value respect even more than love. I saw a lot of interest, excitement, note-taking, and conviction as I shared what our men and our sons see as respect or appreciation—or a lack of it.

Then came the question-and-answer time. A dark-haired woman stood up, and her pretty face was an expressionless mask. "I know you say a man's greatest need is to feel that I respect, trust, and appreciate him. But what if I *don't*?" She explained that her marriage was crumbling due to decisions her husband had made. She no longer respected him, no longer felt admiration or appreciation, and certainly didn't want to take the actions I had just outlined. It was a contentious relationship, and she was feeling pretty hopeless.

In the decade since then, I've interviewed and surveyed thousands of men, women, and teens around the world, and I have heard that dynamic many times—not just about difficult or distant spouses, but also in-laws, colleagues, kids, classmates, parents, teachers, neighbors, whole departments at the office, and rude drivers on the freeway. Every one of us has a relationship (or four) that makes us crazy or that we wish was in a better place. Every one of us also has relationships that we enjoy—and we kind of wish they were all like that. Most of us *want* to be the one who plays well with others, right? We want to get along with those around us.

And sometimes that comes easily. But sometimes it doesn't. We know we should be nicer to a fellow student, reach out to a colleague, or let that rude driver merge without being rude ourselves. We should avoid snapping at our kids, rolling our eyes behind Mom's back, or withholding affection from a spouse. But sometimes we've been so hurt, frustrated, or disrespected, we'd rather vent because it feels good to say what we're really thinking. Sometimes we're just busy and have too many other things on our plate to worry about politeness or managing a challenging relationship. Or sometimes we muster all our self-control and leave the field of play so we *don't* say what's on our minds. We step away and ignore the conflict, throw ourselves into something else to take our minds off of it, call a friend for support, or talk with others who will understand. (We may even seek comfort from our special friends Ben & Jerry.)

Regardless, we're not happy with where the relationship is or where our level of irritation is, but we don't see any path toward change.

That's where this Colorado woman was on that winter day when she acknowledged that although it might be her husband's greatest need, she didn't respect him.

I had no idea how to answer her. So I recommended something I'd heard from author Nancy Leigh DeMoss only a few months before—a challenge to try a particular way of interacting with a husband for one month. I told the woman I was so sorry for the deep struggles in her marriage, explained Nancy's Husband Encouragement Challenge, and suggested that she try it and see what happened. Soon after, we wrapped up the women's conference and I flew home.

"It Changes Everything"

From the moment Nancy shared that challenge with me, it caught my attention. In the years since, I've investigated it in depth, adjusted and added to it, and researched it again.

Three years after that conference, I was in another part of Colorado, speaking at a weekend women's retreat that also included a luncheon with Focus on the Family founder Dr. James Dobson. He spoke for a few minutes and then opened the floor for questions on relationship topics. Near the end, one woman asked, "What if I have shut down in my marriage and just don't like my husband anymore? I know he needs appreciation, I know you say he needs me to trust him, but I can't. What do I do?"

Dr. Dobson looked thoughtful. "Hmm, that's a really good question." Then with a slight twinkle in his eye (since he could have answered her in a heartbeat), he turned to me. "Shaunti?"

Picture me gasping and thinking, *Uh, no pressure!* I gathered my thoughts and looked at this sorrowful woman. "I know this is such a hard time and I'm so sorry. But I do have a suggestion for you, drawn from a thirty-day challenge that we've been researching and experimenting with the last few years. . . ."

After I explained the challenge, she nodded and sat down and another woman stood up. But she didn't ask a question. Instead she turned to the other woman and said, "If you really do that, you'll find it changes everything."

Then she looked at me. "You won't remember me. But three years ago, you came to my church to do a women's conference. My husband and I were in a really bad place. I asked a very similar question and you gave a very similar answer. Everything in me wanted to ignore every word you said. But I also didn't want my kids to grow up in a broken home. So I did it. And it was the beginning of saving our marriage."

As she continued, she started to get teary eyed—and so, I must confess, did I. "My husband and I have worked through so many things. Today we have an amazing relationship. We're not perfect, but we *love* being married. Our kids have a mom and dad who are now committed to each other for life."

KINDNESS IS A BATTLEFIELD

Using the insight of Nancy Leigh DeMoss (now Nancy DeMoss Wolgemuth) as a starting point, and via the seven hundred participants in our research study, we've spent years investigating, refining, testing, and quantifying specific steps that make a huge difference to any relationship. I'll be sharing those in the pages ahead. But when it comes right down to it, the bottom line is pretty simple: *be kind.*

The concept is simple, but that doesn't mean it is effortless, in part because we really don't know how to be kind. You may find that absurd. But I promise you: you almost certainly don't. At least not in the way that works best. And what works best is what I'll be walking you through in this book.

The other reason kindness isn't easy is that it is under siege. We live in an age and culture that have become markedly *un*kind in many ways. People have always had a remarkable capacity for both graciousness and harshness, but today it seems that harshness is more easily let loose.

People today routinely say things over social media, e-mail, and text that they would never utter out loud or face to face. Road-rage confrontations are common. Politicians viciously attack each other, and television news commentators talk over each other. Mean girls openly roll their eyes at school, and bosses feel it is perfectly acceptable to express their disdain at work.

Kindness is easily quashed unless we are purposeful about both protecting and showing it. But we often aren't. On a cultural level, kindness simply isn't a priority today. (Has anyone seen a reality-TV show titled *The Sweetest Housewives of Atlanta* lately?)[1] And on a personal level, our priorities often fight against it! We are encouraged to let our feelings out, to stand up for ourselves, to look out for our rights. We hear statements like "You don't have to take that from him," "You show her who's boss," "You deserve better." Alternatively, we're essentially told to become cold, to back off, to withdraw, to say, "Yes, dear," to hide our feelings here and vent them elsewhere—or to shut off our feelings entirely, suck it up, and check out. Or maybe we're not purposefully cold or checked out, but we're just busy enough that our attention is elsewhere, which amounts to the same thing in the end.

Kindness—true, engaged kindness—takes effort.

But it is also essential. And something inside every one of us is longing for it.

"WHO DOESN'T WANT A KIND HOME?"

As I was conducting an impromptu interview for this book with two business-men in a coffee shop,[2] one of them described the longing for kindness perfectly: "Living in an unkind world is highly dissatisfying. Who doesn't want to come home to a kind home? What kid doesn't want to get off the school bus and meet a kind mother or father? People don't want to work in a hostile workplace—they want to work in a kind one. Not soppy and sentimental, but kind. Every-one wants colleagues who respect them. But the perfect situation, which most people hardly let themselves hope for, is both respectful *and* kind."

I mentioned earlier that in all my years of research, a common denomina-tor in whether people enjoy life is whether they are giving and experiencing kindness (which, for many people, is simply the outward face of unconditional love). When I shared that conclusion with the businessman, I could tell he was wrestling with the thought.

"But I wonder," he mused, "can one really single out kindness as *the* most important thing for enjoying life or enjoying relationships? Why is kindness, as opposed to something else, so important?" He chuckled. "After all, I would really enjoy life a lot if our business took off and I had twenty million dollars rolling in."

His colleague chimed in, "But even then, I'm going to *buy* kindness. I'm going to hire people who are nice to me. All those other things we want are just a means to enjoyment, right? But we won't really enjoy any of them if we can't also get kindness in the bargain. It's another way of saying peace, I think."

The first man said, "Yes, but peace isn't enough. Peace is almost neutral. I think we want more than that. We want actual kindness. That really is it."

A ONE-TWO PUNCH

Why does such a simple tool, *being kind,* bring such dramatic results to restore, build, or improve any relationship we care about? Because it improves how we feel about another person, and it ultimately makes us *want* to be kind.

After all, think about it. Let's say you are irritated with someone (your boss, husband, wife, mother-in-law, teenager). If you tell that person you're irritated and then you tell someone else you're irritated, are you going to be more or less irritated? The answer is obvious. And yet, what if you're irritated but you don't talk about it? What if instead you set out every day to be kind to them and about them—to find, for example, something positive or praiseworthy about that person—and then you tell them and tell someone else? Are you going to be more or less irritated? Also obvious!

When one of my corporate clients, Nadia, heard what this book was about, she told me of her experience years ago working in a new city with a harsh boss, and how she regularly wanted to vent with another colleague who also bore the brunt of their boss's poor management style. But the colleague would have none of it.

"If you are negative," she said to Nadia, "does it really change anything in the end?"

"Well, it sure feels good to vent all the frustrations," Nadia responded. "But no, I guess it doesn't really change anything."

"You're wrong." Her colleague leaned in. "It does change something. It changes you."

Nadia was so struck by that, she began to watch and emulate her colleague. This woman was very successful in business, but Nadia saw more than that. She saw graciousness in the face of harshness. Generosity in the face of stinginess. Patience when their boss was exasperated. She saw someone she wanted to be.

Practicing kindness made Nadia want to be kind.

As I listened to the qualities of Nadia's colleague, I found myself wishing I myself was so much more like that. In fact, the description reminded me of someone else. I don't know whether Nadia or her colleague embrace a Christian faith, but as I listened, I couldn't help but think, *This sounds like the way the Bible describes Jesus.* (I should mention that although my research is scientifically rigorous and applies to readers across all demographics, including race, age, and religion, I also do quite a bit of work in the church community. Many of my books bring in faith-based applications—including this one, since kindness is famously central to the teachings of Jesus.)

In a well-known sermon recounted in the gospel of Luke, Jesus called out, "Love your enemies! Do good to those who hate you. . . . Lend to them without expecting to be repaid. Then your reward from heaven will be very great, and you will truly be acting as children of the Most High, for he is kind to those who are unthankful and wicked."[3]

And the research shows that as we similarly show that kindness—even when it is undeserved—something changes. Not necessarily in the other person, not yet, but in us.

That is the most basic and important change that occurred in the life of that woman in Colorado. As she started to be purposeful about looking for the positives in her husband and avoiding the tendency to focus on the negatives, her "But what if I don't respect him?" question went away. She started to notice those things that were worthy of praise but for which she hadn't really given him credit. The problems didn't loom quite as large in her eyes. She started to feel a sense of appreciation for and trust in her husband again. She began to want to show him the respect I had been talking about and that he so needed.

She wasn't the only person who changed. Her husband responded less defensively and opened up more to give what she needed. And the positive cycle continued. Her new mind-set, words, and actions didn't magically solve some other very real problems, but those steps sure made the problems easier to deal with.

She discovered the power of kindness. And you can too.

Ready? I'll show you how.

THE 30-DAY KINDNESS CHALLENGE

If kindness is really a power-packed means of transforming relationships, how can we put it to work? I've mentioned a tool called the 30-Day Kindness Challenge. It is designed to build a sustainable desire for and habit in each of three key aspects of kindness: avoiding negativity, finding and praising the positive, and performing kind actions that matter to someone else. There are also some important alterations for specific groups of people (in particular, men doing this for their wives), which I'll cover a bit later. But here is the primary challenge.

Pick someone with whom you want or need a better relationship. And for the next thirty days do the following:

1. Say nothing negative about your person, either to them or about them to someone else. (If negative feedback is unavoidable—such as when you as a boss, teacher, coach, or parent need to address a mistake—be constructive and encouraging without a negative tone.)

2. Every day, find one positive thing that you can sincerely praise or affirm about your person and tell them, and tell someone else.

3. Every day, do a small act of kindness or generosity for your person.

That's it. So simple. But the three aspects of kindness are like three chemical elements that, when they come together, react and build something different: something remarkably beautiful, powerful, and, above all, transformative.

In our research, no matter who did the Challenge or on whom they were focused—a romantic partner, colleague, stepparent, child—as long as participants practiced those three habits, 89 percent saw improvement in their relationships. The graph below shows results for those who did the Challenge for a spouse, boyfriend, or girlfriend.

Simple Changes, Big Results*

Do you believe your relationship improved as a result of the 30-Day Kindness Challenge?

Yes, there is a distinct, noticeable improvement. (For example: we are definitely closer, or we argue less or let things go more, or…)	42.7%
Yes, there is general improvement, although it is hard to pin down what has specifically changed.	46.7%
Total Improved	**89.3%**
No, our relationship hasn't improved.	10.7%

You may be thinking, *Okay, so if all I need to do to take the Kindness Challenge is to follow these three steps, why am I holding a whole book about it? What else could I possibly need to know?*

Embarking on the 30-Day Kindness Challenge with no additional input is a bit like rebuilding a damaged house with no outside help. Wouldn't it be way better to rebuild that house with advice from seasoned friends, a few targeted DIY videos, and maybe even a contractor or two? You'll be far more effective and productive when an experienced friend works beside you and says, for example, "You may not realize it, but behind that panel are two pipes, so make sure you cut here instead of there."

This book works the same way (as do our daily reminder e-mails, self-assessment quizzes, and other resources you can find at JoinTheKindness Challenge.com). And as you'll see in the chapters ahead, all of us need this coaching because there are so many ways we're simply blind to how kind or

---

* Unless otherwise noted, all survey charts in this book show results among those who did the 30-Day Kindness Challenge for a romantic partner for two weeks or more.

unkind we actually are. For example, if I asked in what ways you are regularly negative toward others, you might say, "I'm not!" right up until the moment you go through chapter 6.

In the chapters ahead, you'll discover specific patterns to look for that might be sabotaging your relationships without your even realizing it. And you'll learn simple adjustments that will eliminate the bad patterns and boost the good ones. Most of us think we're pretty good at figuring out how we're doing at relationships, and yet kindness blindness may be tripping us up. I've spent quite a few years on the research to help us be able to identify our individual blind spots (so we can fix them) and opportunities (so we can seize them). If you want to learn more about the research, see the methodology chapter online at JoinTheKindnessChallenge.com or at my main website, Shaunti.com.

In short, the pages ahead will help you uncover the ways you're good or bad at practicing relationship-altering kindness and support your DIY process to build the house right.

Kindness Is a Superpower

A Little Kindness Goes a Long Way

Do you want a better life? *Be kind.* Want a better relationship with someone? *Be kind.* Want a more profitable business, a happier mind-set, a meaningful impact, a better sex life, or for people to respect and enjoy you? *Be kind.*

It almost seems too good to be true. Like something an old-time huckster would try to sell you at the state fair: a one-size-fits-all solution for every problem! And yet . . . it kind of is. Realistically, of course, it won't solve *every* problem, and it's certainly not one-size-fits-all, since everyone will apply it differently. But I've been doing this research for more than ten years, and I have seen a consistent truth: kindness is a superpower. It is explosive, supernatural, and transformational. True kindness always strengthens and empowers, never weakens. It changes you, not just others. It melts hardness and makes gentleness immensely powerful.

Kindness has a power to transform that is unparalleled in social science.

For years, a well-known technology company (which I will call Global) organized many large and high-visibility events around the world. These events were extremely popular with the attendees but not with the sponsors, vendors, and other businesses involved. In fact, about five years ago, as I was doing some research for my business books, a longtime major sponsor actually brought up Global as an example of a business with an extraordinarily valuable audience, but which was so frustrating to work with that it was no longer worth it. Shortly thereafter, the company discontinued their sponsorship.

Several years later, Global's president moved on. Within two years under new leadership, multiple sponsors had returned and event attendance was rising. I sat down with the new president to hear what had changed. Look at his description:

> As I was coming on board, our reputation was an attitude that said, "You're lucky to work with us." We were the cool kids. We had an edge to us that was uncomfortable. We were exclusive and proud of that. And the sponsors knew they needed to be in front of our audience, but they hated working with us.
>
> We had a culture of a lack of service. Not just customer service, but *service*. We didn't serve our sponsors. Onsite at events we were in demand, we were impatient, we were rubbing shoulders with the celebrities who were our speakers. And we were almost celebrities ourselves in some ways. Not to mention that event planners are Type A and our to-do lists are long, so if a sponsor had a problem and we were frustrated at the interruption, then we were signaling *they* were the problem. Regardless, we sure weren't focused on serving those who needed it.
>
> Offsite, our attitude was that we win every deal, we get the best of everything, and if you don't want to work with us that's fine because there's a line of people outside that door who do.
>
> Bottom line: over time, we found that it is not enough for sponsors to want to be in front of our audience—they have to want to work with us. Sponsors want to enjoy an event too. And ours hated it.
>
> The encouraging thing is how quickly you can turn your reputa-

tion around. How do you do that? You're kind. You're warm. You're gracious. Every time we have a big event now, I tell my team, "You've done all the work and planning. So now as a staff member, you have two jobs. One is to serve your guts out. There is not a single person you interact with who is an interruption to your day. Everyone here is the reason we do the things we do. And job number two is to have fun."

Both are important, but kindness is the starting and ending point. Fun leads to kindness, and being kind leads to everyone having a lot more fun.

That focus has changed us. We're still as exclusive as we've ever been. I still have to say no to sponsors who want to do certain things. But it is a signal of our massive progress that we have more sponsors who are spending more money than they've ever spent. And they *want* to. Literally, I will hear it fifteen or thirty times an event: "Man, this doesn't even feel like the same organization, the same staff!"

And that's the cool thing: it *is* largely the same staff. But the leaders now set the tone for a culture of kindness. We tell everyone, "This is what the culture will be. You don't have an option. If you're sitting here in staff meetings, then you're agreeing to a specific standard of behavior. You're agreeing to choose to value relationships." Hit your markers, yes. Deliver results. But if kindness is missing, you can deliver results but you won't have real trust. I've seen it over and over: if you choose relationships over results you get better results in the long run.

There is a night-and-day difference now. This is not a short-term switch to get people back in. This is the long-term strategy. We are now a company that exists to serve people, rather than existing to be served.

And that is why we transitioned some folks out—because that was not their style. They were just toxic to the organization. Some people simply aren't kind, even after seeing the impact it has. I don't get it. Kindness makes life much better.

THE SUPERPOWERS OF KINDNESS

Whether you are eight or eighty, a senior corporate executive or a high-school student, a spouse or single, an inner-city single parent just trying to survive or a wealthy business owner, kindness makes life much better.

How? What sort of powers does it really have? And more to the point, what power will it offer us in our relationships? Let's make like any elated new superhero (think Spider-Man, the Flash, or Johnny Storm) and examine the powers kindness gives us to make life better—for us and for those around us.

Kindness Makes You Bulletproof

Think of a situation that really bugs you, one in which you are tempted to be unkind; even if you don't actually say something mean, you're likely thinking it. Maybe it is whenever your ex-wife criticizes your lateness in picking up the kids and you want to issue a stinging retort. Perhaps it is your teenage daughter's eye-roll or your classmate's derisive tone that's guaranteed to make your head explode.

Whatever pushes your buttons is an emotional bullet; it hits you right where it hurts.

Kindness has the power to make those bullets bounce off. By your predetermination to be unconditionally kind to your ex-wife, your classmate, or the people you come across—especially when they don't deserve it—suddenly you have control of your feelings. You have taken away their power to make you crazy.

As one of my friends told me years ago when she was describing a consistently mean neighbor, "I'm not going to let him bust my peace."

My husband, Jeff, has joined me in a great deal of research and has seen how this works in many people's lives, including his own. As a committed rule follower, it makes him a bit crazy when people blatantly break either stated regulations or the rules of common courtesy. But as he points out, kindness has this strange ability to change his inner angst:

I think about when I'm driving on the highway. My job, of course, is to enforce the rules of the road on behalf of all civilized society. So when two lanes are merging into one and everyone has waited their turn for a half a mile, and there's that inevitable jerk who speeds all the way up to the end and tries to squeeze in, I'm so irritated. And there is some satisfaction in preventing him from doing that. But it doesn't make me feel any less stressed or on edge than I was before. And quite frankly, if I'm a jerk in response, it doesn't feel great.

But if I decide in advance that I'm just not going to stand on my rights in that type of situation and instead I'm going to react kindly, something changes. The next time that event rolls around, or whenever someone wrongs me, the stress and anxiety of it roll off. I might still stand up for what is right, especially if it is on behalf of others. But being kind about it guarantees that I'll be able to move beyond that initial anger and that incident quickly, as opposed to getting stuck in mulling over it.

The bullet hit, but it bounced off.

Kindness Disarms the Attacker

In the Marvel Universe, several characters disarm attacks by absorbing whatever negative energy is thrown at them and sending it back in a different way. The attacker is essentially rendered impotent. Well, a positive version of that process exists in real life. All our research, and social science in general, has found that when someone is being verbally harangued or ridiculed and actively responds in the opposite spirit, there's a high likelihood of not just transforming the attack but the attacker.

One young man I interviewed had spent the previous year keeping his temper in check when someone ticked him off. He described the revelation he experienced shortly thereafter:

I was backing out of my parking space at the gym and not paying enough attention. This lady was speeding down the aisle and I almost creamed her. I stopped suddenly and made all the hand gestures that said, "Oops. My bad. I'm so sorry." But she stopped her car, backed up, and proceeded to tell me at very high volume how reckless and dangerous it was for me to pull out without seeing if a car was coming. I responded uncharacteristically: "You are absolutely right. I was so in the wrong. Please forgive me. Are you okay?"

She looked at me for a beat and then said, "Oh. Yes. It's fine. It's okay. I was just in a hurry because . . ."

She had been spewing all this vitriol and suddenly she had nothing left to throw at me. And because I absorbed the anger and responded with kindness, she absorbed the kindness and responded the same way.

Kindness Gives You X-Ray Vision

Who hasn't wished they could know what another person was thinking? Looking through physical walls is one thing, but who hasn't wanted to peer inside someone's mind and heart and figure out what is going on in there?

When I first began interviewing the people who had taken the 30-Day Kindness Challenge, I was startled to hear many of them describe that exact dynamic. The act of forcing themselves not to be negative, to find and say praiseworthy things, and to be generous each day had an unexpected side effect: they suddenly were attuned to the other person's point of view. Without really intending to, they found that they were putting themselves in the other person's shoes.

One young wife told me she had been arguing with her husband about why he had spent a portion of their tax refund instead of saving it since they were already in debt. She had said her piece several times. One evening during the 30-Day Kindness Challenge she noticed an earlier purchase on their bank statement and pointed out yet again, "This was a bad decision."

And he said, "Why do you keep saying that? I know I made a mistake!"

She continued the story:

So I left the room. Then I realized I'd messed up on the "say nothing negative" part of the Challenge and tried to think of something positive. Suddenly I felt terrible. It was as if I saw myself through his eyes: *Here is my wife, who has said this before two or three times. And I already know I screwed up, and I feel bad. Yet here she is again, calling me irresponsible.*

I realized he really must think that I think he's irresponsible! Yet he's the furthest thing from it. We disagree about money, but he's a great husband and he works so hard, and he's a great dad. But I think I've caused him to believe he's somehow not enough. I suddenly saw that I really get on him about things like money or about not giving me his full attention. See, he works with teenagers and when he comes home he has to catch up on their text messages, and they're blowing up his phone, so when I go to talk to him it's like talking to a brick wall.

And then I realized something else: he probably doesn't want to have to deal with all those text messages either!

By this point I felt doubly awful since I know he needs my affirmation, not criticism. I knew I had to apologize. I said, "I'm sorry for pointing that out again. I know you care about our finances. You provide so well for our family." And when he heard me say that, I could just tell that I got his attention. He even put down his phone, and we had this amazing conversation. I wasn't talking to a brick wall anymore because he knew I saw his heart.

Kindness Melts Through Walls

Not long ago I had dinner with a group of female executives. When they asked about my next research project and learned that one goal of this book was to help transform difficult relationships, a woman described a highly contentious situation with her longtime boyfriend's twenty-two-year-old daughter. The female executive saw the daughter as incredibly self-centered and indicated that the younger woman saw her as judgmental. And the one factor that made this executive unwilling to marry her boyfriend was that the daughter still lived at home. In other words, this one difficult relationship was having a pretty out-sized impact on her life.

When she asked what the research would suggest she do, I explained the 30-Day Kindness Challenge. And with my very first words ("For the next month, don't say anything negative about his daughter, either to her or about her to anyone else"), she groaned. "Oh man, I don't know if that is possible! But go on, what's the rest?" When I finished, she looked thoughtful. "I'll be honest. That sounds really tough. But what I've been doing up until now obviously hasn't worked. Maybe it's time to try something new."

I left that dinner thinking that if she did indeed take the hard steps of spending one month nixing the negativity, finding something each day to praise, and doing small acts of kindness, she would be shocked at the difference it made and wish she had tried it a lot sooner. It is only when you are actively kind to someone who is not kind to you that you see the true power of Christ-like kindness.

You see, when we have contentious or difficult relationships with people, they typically build a barrier—like a castle wall—to protect their hearts. They might be wary or simply on edge. They have their defenses up because they expect flaming arrows of anger, sneers of indifference, or jolts of sarcasm, criticism, micromanagement, or judgment. But then imagine that your anger, sarcasm, or judgmental attitude disappears and you are suddenly kind and affirming instead. That action doesn't break down the walls the other person had built; it melts them. It is as if those kind words or actions slip straight through the defenses and directly touch their heart. The other person didn't "let you in"; it just happened. Because kindness has that superpower. And it is even more powerful coming from what they see as an unlikely source.

Of course, they can shake it off, harden their hearts, throw whatever touched their hearts into the castle moat, and brick the wall back into place. They can ignore you or choose to believe the worst of you. But that's the point:

remaining negative about you takes work. If you continue to be kind, your actions will keep melting the wall and the other person will have to keep putting those bricks back up.

This is why we've seen that at some point, many people finally let their defenses stay down. They begin to trust that we mean what we are saying through our consistent kindness. They begin to believe that maybe we aren't going to shred their hearts. The wall against us is gone. And now, of course, we have a responsibility to be true to that trust.

Kindness Springs Open Locked Doors

Some people become locked in a dungeon of bitterness, shame, hostility, or anger, and it impacts how they interact with everyone around them. One of the hardest times to be kind is also one of the most powerful: when we treat someone well who, for no reason, is *not* treating us well. Unlike the previous example, we haven't been rude or judgmental, but the person lashes out anyway. Yet when we answer unkindness with grace and harshness with gentleness, those actions don't just preserve our peace of mind; they transform theirs. In time, those actions can set them free from the prison in which they've been trapped.

Now, just to be clear, we cannot actually change someone else's mind or heart. But God can. And I believe the great and mysterious superpower of kindness to soften a hard or angry heart is actually the outward evidence of God working behind the scenes.

Lori saw that firsthand. Her mother-in-law, Peggy, was the most cantankerous, critical person she knew. And unfortunately, because Peggy was a widow and physically infirm, she had to live with Lori and her husband, Evan. She moved in when the couple had been married for only eight years and had three young kids. From the first moment, Peggy shared her critical opinions of Lori's housekeeping, cooking, and mothering. Lori and Evan tried every conceivable way of addressing it, including establishing boundaries ("Mom, if what I cook isn't working for you, let's arrange it so you can cook for yourself"). When even boundaries didn't work, Lori had to decide: *Do I keep on letting her drive me crazy? Or do I treat her the way I wish she would treat me—even though she doesn't?*

She prayed about it, asked God for strength to do the impossible, and set about trying to be kind to her mother-in-law. Every day. Month after month. Year after year. No matter what Peggy said, Lori gave a gentle answer. No matter how negative Peggy was ("I can't believe Sarah was so noisy in the grocery store!"), Lori was resolutely positive ("It is hard when a toddler sees something she wants, isn't it? I was proud of the older two for being so polite, though."). When Peggy was cruel ("You're raising these kids in a barn. They deserve better."), Lori would call her on it and tell her it was inappropriate but then banish the cruel words from her mind and try to carry on as if Peggy hadn't said a thing.

Lori said, "There's only one reason I was able to do this: a straight miracle from God. I asked him for the strength and love. And he gave it to me. That is the only explanation."

Nearly five years later, without warning, a switch flipped. Lori began to notice that Peggy was softer. Instead of complaining about everything, she started saying thank you. She started noticing the little gestures of kindness Lori had made all along that Peggy had never recognized, much less appreciated. She started smiling more. She began to listen to a well-known pastor on the radio and took his words to heart. And one day she asked Lori and Evan if they could help her find God for herself.

Within a few short weeks, Peggy was a different person. Where she used to wear a permanent scowl, now she had a twinkle in her eye. Where she once constantly complained about her increasing disability, now she talked about all the things she could still do.

Evan said, "If we ever wanted proof of the power of Jesus to radically transform a life, this was it. Mom went from being the most negative person I knew to the most hopeful. In fact, every night when Lori would say, 'Good night, Mom, see you in the morning,' my mom used to say, 'What's good about it?' or even, 'Maybe I'll die in my sleep and take myself off your hands.' Within a few weeks of this transformation, Lori would say, 'See you in the morning,' and my mother would get this chipper tone in her voice and say, 'I hope, I hope!' It was remarkable. And it was all about God using Lori's extreme patience and kindness. She just wore her down!"

Kindness Passes Along Its Power

Years ago I saw a character on a sci-fi television series who could pass along his superpower by purposefully touching his target. Some of those people could then transfer it to others, and so on. As a result, that power began to pop up everywhere.

Kindness does something similar. It sets off a chain reaction. It replicates itself. It goes viral. In a beautiful, miraculous way, it spreads by transforming those it touches so they become carriers and pass it along. Many of those who tested the 30-Day Kindness Challenge described seeing the person they were being kind to suddenly become more gentle, caring, and attentive to others. Many others realized that they themselves had become sort of super-carriers: they were spreading kindness in all directions without really intending to.

Before she started the 30-Day Kindness Challenge, one anonymous survey taker described a difficult situation at work:

> I am doing the 30-Day Kindness Challenge for my immediate supervisor. She can be very manipulative and passive aggressive. She regularly takes credit for my work and dumps all the responsibilities she doesn't enjoy onto me simply because she can. I've been told by HR that she sees me as a threat to her job, and not as another teammate. But I want her to feel less insecure around me. I'm not trying to take her job. I want a healthy work relationship with her.

Thirty days later, although the situation as a whole wasn't resolved, the survey taker said, "There has been a noted improvement in the overall health of the relationship." But then she explained an unexpected side effect: "I also noticed a huge change in the way I interact with others. I found that I was more focused on how I could show kindness to others I interact with daily. Since I was focused on thinking of ways to be engaged in the Kindness Challenge with my target, it was pretty natural to just let that carry over to others around me."[1]

As I read or listened to many accounts like hers, I realized that when two parties are fighting—whether on a physical battleground or within marriage, community, business, or politics—that type of unkindness inevitably hurts innocent bystanders; an outcome known as collateral damage. But when someone is trying to be kind instead, there appears to be collateral benefit. They're targeting one person with kindness, and it has a positive impact on many others.

As one man put it, "With collateral damage, you can't identify whom your actions are going to affect. Just the same, when you set off the kindness bomb, you have no idea where it is going to go and whom it is going to positively impact with its shock wave."

Kindness Makes the Invisible Visible

When you start looking for ways to be kind, it often means looking for ways to affirm another person. This is an interesting twist, because if you've been in a contentious relationship, the negative things have probably loomed large and you may have seen little or nothing positive.

But we've discovered that once you start actively being kind by *looking* for the positives, you'll see them clearly. They aren't new; they were there the whole time. But it is as if many traits, actions, words, and attributes are invisible to us, and through our practicing kindness, they are suddenly revealed.

Even more telling is what else is sometimes revealed: the hidden inner insecurities and fears that could account for negative behavior.

One mom described an insight she gained as she was doing the 30-Day Kindness Challenge for her sixteen-year-old son. "He thinks the world revolves around him. He's not mouthy to other people, but he is to the family. He's an amazing student and does well at his job. He's not a rebel. But at home his arrogance is hard to handle." Then she added, "But sometimes now, I see under that. I see that his attitude is just a mask for his insecurity, just as it is for most people who are arrogant. And I also see moments that I might have missed before, when he lets me in and I see that he loves me."

One young man shared a similar story about his older brother with whom he had a strained relationship. He concluded, "Underneath that surface is doubt and insecurity. I know that is the case for me. Once I started looking past that irritating front, once I tried to speak to and be kind to that softer person who is there on the inside, I started seeing that person more. And I also started to see a lot more of the good stuff that I was too irritated to notice before. It made a big difference to be able to see those things and then to be able to say something about them."

Kindness Keeps Powering You

If there were a superpower that kept making its host better and faster the more the host used it, this would be it. I don't know if that exists in the comic-book pantheon, but this kindness power is clear in real life. As you apply kindness, you enjoy life more. You also want to be more kind. Which makes you enjoy life more. And so on, in a self-powering cycle.

Recently I asked one of my best friends how her daughter's marriage was going, since the young couple had just celebrated their first anniversary. My friend chuckled and said,

> I just asked them that same thing yesterday. My daughter said, "He is so kind. For example, some husbands would demand that their wife wear some sexy little thing in the evening and yet there I sit in my giant robe, with my hair up in a towel, watching TV and laughing, with a plate of cookies on my lap. And he just smiles at me."
>
> So I asked her husband, "How is it that you can be so kind about everything?"

He said, "It's easy. I look at her sitting there so content and laughing, and I think, I'm so happy she's happy. In some way that has to reflect well on me! So knowing I'm doing a good job makes *me* happy. So if I'm kind, and it makes both of us happy, it just works all the way around."

My friend concluded, "People need to know there's definitely a little bit of enlightened self-interest in being kind!"

Kindness Requires Heroic Self-Sacrifice

Finally, we need to acknowledge the sobering reality faced by every superhero: using our superpower requires self-sacrifice, not self-protection.

For example, many of us instinctively try to make our lives better by insisting on fair treatment. While fairness is a great goal in some ways, insisting on it rarely makes us happier. In fact, ironically, the reverse is true. Our lives and relationships will never be happy without kindness. And *we can't be kind without being willing to give up our rights.* We can't be kind without self-sacrifice.

Remember the sermon by Jesus I mentioned in the previous chapter? Well, in that passage Jesus was saying, essentially, why should we get a pat on the back when we are nice to someone who is nice to us? That part is easy—after all, even someone who is a complete jerk does that.[2] What is hard, he pointed out, is being kind and gracious to the complete jerk. In saying "Love your enemies!" and "Do good to those who hate you," Jesus challenged his audience (and each of us!) to do exactly that. In fact, the Golden Rule of "Do to others as you would like them to do to you" comes from this moment in Jesus's message.[3] In context, that famous phrase essentially means, "Treat someone who is not kind to you in the kind and generous way you wish they were treating you."

That person with whom we want a good (or at least a better) relationship may not be a complete jerk; he or she may in fact be a great person we care about very much. But regardless of how that person treats us, Jesus urges us to treat him or her kindly and well. Not only because that honors God with our lives but because that sacrificial action has power.

Kindness is the unspoken result of the Golden Rule. And the power of kindness is a prerequisite for transforming relationships.

You may be skeptical of that notion or even worried that kindness may at times let people off the hook when holding the line is needed instead. Let's look at those concerns next.

Is Kindness Ever the Wrong Approach?

And Other Concerns

t would be natural to be politely skeptical of the claims made so far. (Or perhaps, despite the theme of this book, not so politely skeptical!) Let's briefly examine some common concerns.

DON'T OTHER FACTORS MATTER AS MUCH AS KINDNESS?

You may wonder whether kindness is really a prerequisite for better relationships. Don't other factors matter too? Yes, of course! Kindness is not the only quality needed for improving our relationships. After all, I've spent ten years and hundreds of thousands of research dollars investigating the missing *knowledge* we need in order to give others what they need—which is also absolutely crucial for great relationships. Knowledge and kindness go hand in hand. Being kind is empty if you're trying to be kind in all the wrong areas. And knowing what to do is empty if you don't do it with kindness.

We'll dive into this a bit more in chapter 7, but here's an example. A wife can be purposeful about saying "I love you" to her husband several times a day.

But if what he really needs is to feel appreciated (for example, for his efforts to fix the kitchen sink) and she unintentionally signals the opposite ("While you were in there, why didn't you put on a new faucet?"), her kindness efforts won't hit the mark! Or suppose a husband knows his wife needs to feel listened to, and he does listen, but in a functional, get-to-the-point sort of way, his efforts will not hit the mark.

So what we see in the research is this profound reality: kindness is certainly not the only factor that matters, but you cannot improve a relationship, a group dynamic, or a culture without it. Period.

And here's why. Two people form a relationship. You cannot change the other person; you can change only yourself. As I've mentioned, showing kindness to the other person *impacts* the other person and *changes* you. And as we'll demonstrate in the pages ahead, the kinder you are, the more you want to be kind. And then your kindness usually makes the other person want to change! That change of heart often leads them to change how they interact, to be more kind themselves. And so on in a virtuous cycle. You can see in the chart on the next page that three out of four who did the 30-Day Kindness Challenge for a romantic partner (and two out of three who did it for any other type of relationship) said that although they were the ones doing the hard work, they saw their targets change for the better!

And that is just one example of how often people grow and change when they are on the receiving end of kindness. In one way or another, it nearly always has an impact. But I know some questions or skepticism remain. Let's briefly examine a couple of common concerns.

Is Kindness Ever the Wrong Approach?

One businessman in a focus group voiced a common skepticism this way: "Is kindness essential? Much of the time, yes. Even most of the time. But always? No. That guy at the car repair shop who lied to you, who ripped you off—you don't need to be kind to him. You need to confront him. It seems as though kindness is a principle for interpersonal relationships, not professional or vendor relationships. It is not a cure-all in every situation."

Another person in the focus group spoke up: "Yes, but I would say you could and should be kind rather than unkind in confronting the person. The car repair guy has already ripped you off; don't let him rob you of your emotional health as well. And even if you are confronting him very directly and clearly, your kindness now is extending to the person you don't know. Because you've called this guy out on it, he may not do it to the next person in line."

You Change, They Change

As you think about your partner's development as a person, do you think they have changed for the better or worse in the last few months? "I think…"

They have changed a bit for the better.	35%
They have changed a lot for the better.	39%
They've changed for the better.	**74%**
They are about the same / they haven't changed.	23%
No change.	**23%**
They have changed a lot for the worse.	1%
They have changed a little for the worse.	2%
They've changed for the worse.	**3%**
Total	**100%**

Now remember, this practice creates good relationships with those people in our lives whom we care about; you may not feel that that extends to the dishonest car repair guy! For me, though, it does. I feel a weight of responsibility from God's command to "love your enemies" as well as his admonition, "If it is possible, as far as it depends on you, live at peace with everyone."[1] Which means I feel called to handle the situation with as much kindness as I can when I'm talking to the dishonest car repair guy . . . or the exasperating telephone customer service representative who takes an hour instead of ten minutes to solve a simple problem on my credit card account . . . or the completely incompetent driver who cuts me off in traffic.

Hmm. Clearly this is something I'm still working on.

WHEN IS STRENGTH NEEDED INSTEAD?

But aren't there cases where kindness could undermine efforts to improve a relationship? After all, in troubled relationships aren't discipline, strength, boundaries, and even hard words sometimes needed instead? Absolutely. But *if those approaches are truly needed,* then by definition those words and actions, handled with care, are usually the kindest thing you can do.

Here we must make an absolutely crucial distinction: being kind is not the same thing as being nice, keeping the peace, and not rocking the boat. There's nothing wrong with being nice—it can make for a much more pleasant environment—but it is shallower than being kind.

Kindness cares about the best interests of others, and so it doesn't shy away from a challenge. Niceness, by contrast, may or may not be motivated by caring about the other person at a deep level. In fact, when niceness is our goal, we can easily avoid conflict because our priority is keeping a pleasant atmosphere rather than addressing issues that need attention. One business leader put it this way:

I'd say that niceness is a by-product of kindness, but niceness on its own isn't the goal. Kindness will challenge others when it sees something wrong, but it does so in gentleness and hopefulness. Niceness avoids difficult conversations because that might upset the desire for a lack of conflict. That's one reason many people see niceness in others as a phony outward display. But true kindness is the farthest thing from phony. It requires honesty and strength.

For example, suppose you are at your wit's end because an adult child isn't getting treatment for alcohol addiction. Refusing to make excuses or help her out of the latest jam may feel really unkind in the moment, but it actually isn't. Or if your colleague is inappropriately harsh with other coworkers, stating hard truths or bringing about workplace discipline may feel unkind, but it isn't. In most cases, *not* doing those things would merely enable those people to destroy themselves and put at risk something that greatly matters to them (their marriage, your friendship, their job, and so on). If you know something must change—not for your sake, but for theirs—then as Dave Ramsey often says, "To be unclear is to be unkind."

Further, taking those steps of strength is often the only means of preventing unkindness to others.

Whether or not you dive into a difficult situation isn't the issue; what makes you either kind or unkind is how you express it. Remember the goals: improving the relationship and bringing about heart change. If the actions you take aren't simply to make the other person feel bad or eliminate him or her from your life, then you need to take those actions with a sense of great care. Combating unkindness with unkindness defeats the purpose! Worse, anything done out of frustration, hurt, or anger is likely to achieve only defensiveness and a worse relationship.

So yes, refuse to bail out the prodigal child after her third car accident. But make this clear: "I will help you get a job so you can pay off the repairs." Confront your colleague about his harsh words being inappropriate and say that if it happens again you'll need to report it to HR, but be calm and polite throughout and add a phrase like, "I know you don't intend to be cruel."

After all, ask yourself: *If I were in that person's shoes, which approach would be more likely to not just open my eyes but also change my heart?*

IF AT FIRST YOU DON'T SUCCEED . . .

Although kindness is essential for any relationship we want to improve, we have all seen many ways the process can break down. We are imperfect people and we will never do it right all the time. Despite our best intentions, we may be unkind. We may withhold affection, snap at the other person, assume the worst of their good intentions, hold on to unforgiveness, apply boundaries incorrectly, and so on. The other person may never come to that place of wanting to change. Or even if they do, they may not understand the right thing to do and thus try all sorts of changes that don't matter to us or don't work. Or we might try changes that don't matter or don't work. The possibilities for derailing that virtuous cycle are endless.

But most of the time kindness works. Why? Well, we've joked about kindness being a superpower, but in truth I do think something deeply supernatural happens through it, something that comes from God's using our words and actions in a special and unique way. When we are willing to step outside ourselves; lay down our rights, busyness, hurts, frustrations, and irritations; and extend to others what the Bible calls loving-kindness, it changes the situation. It changes people.

After all, according to the Bible, God has an almost inconceivable number of wonderful attributes—but of all of them, God's kindness is described as the quality that reaches into our hearts, leads us to feel bad for what we've done wrong, and drives true change. As the apostle Paul wrote to the church in Rome, "Don't you see how wonderfully kind, tolerant, and patient God is with you? . . . Can't you see that his kindness is intended to turn you from your sin?"[2]

God is that way with us. And he asks us to be that way with others.

Kindness in Practice

Put It to Work

Here's where you break out your DIY kindness kit and figure out how it works in practice. We've already seen the superpowers of kindness; now we need to know how to use them.

Kindness is not some esoteric idea floating out in the ether; it is an ultra-practical tool—a *power tool,* so to speak. Just as with any specialized tool you would use to repair a house, test a student's reading ability, or deliver medicine in the right dosage, you need to know how this tool of kindness actually functions in practice if you're going to use it well in your life—both over the short term (such as in the 30-Day Kindness Challenge) and to create a new lifestyle of kindness for the long term.

So here are eight principals about how kindness works with most people in most situations.

1. Kindness Doesn't Happen Naturally

We are busy people living in a stressful world. So if we aren't being purposeful about something important—like, say, improving relationships—we just don't think about it. Or we are stumped by what to do. Either way, it is all too easy to do nothing and hope it gets better on its own. Either way, our default is inertia. And because we are imperfect people, inertia doesn't usually equal kindness!

As one woman said before she started the 30-Day Kindness Challenge, "I realize I need to find ways to be kind, because I sure can't make it come naturally these days."

If we're going to be kind, there is no choice but to be purposeful about it. Think of anything else you do that is crucial to your day-to-day ability to keep functioning. Filling up your car with gas. Getting groceries. Doing homework. Changing your child's diaper. (That one is particularly crucial.) Paying your rent. In each area, you've learned that if you don't take those actions there will be pain. So you plan for these actions and do them consistently. In other words, you are purposeful.

Kindness is like that. You must be just as purposeful to avoid the pain. Even better, as mentioned earlier, if you are purposeful you'll be amazed at how much more you love your life.

But what if you don't *want* to be purposeful? What if you really, honestly don't want to be kind in this particular relationship—even if you know you should?

One friend of mine comes from an unusually difficult background and yet has the best attitude. She is always laughing, encouraging others, and praying for people, and she has been elevated into the public eye and many positions of influential leadership in national initiatives because she is not only smart, capable, and funny, but she's kind.

Recently I connected with her during breakfast at a conference. We talked a bit about this book and I asked, "What is your secret?" She didn't hesitate:

I often mentor younger women whose marriages are in trouble or whose lives or businesses are falling apart. I tell them to remember one thing and say it to themselves over and over: Obedience precedes emotion.

What is God asking of you? Do it. Even if you don't feel it. Because then you *will* feel it later.

Just two days ago one woman told me, "I can't forgive my husband." And there are some real issues there. But she has to forgive her husband, or it is all going to fall apart. And frankly, she's not helping matters by what she is focusing on and talking about over and over. I said, "I hear you, girlfriend, and you're right, you probably can't forgive him by yourself. You are running on empty. So you need to invite the power of the Holy Spirit into this right now. That is your fuel. That has to be poured into the tank before you even start the car toward forgiveness."

She said, "Okay, but then what?" And I gave her the Elly May Clampett version and said, "Then you have to shut the piehole. You are sabotaging him, your marriage, and your own heart with every frustrated word you say to him and others. And the more you are negative, the harder it will be to forgive. But guess what? The more you are present in the present, the more you let obedience to God precede your emotion, the easier it will get. You may not feel right now like loving him, being kind to him, and praying for him, but just do it."

I've had many issues in my own marriage, in my own life. I know it works. Your choice starts the process. I told her, "You have to start somewhere, and this is it. You have to be receptive, forgiving, and kind." She said, "But it's not changing him!" And I said, "You're right. But it is changing *you*. And the change in your heart has the ability to change the atmosphere in the room. And then *that* changes his heart. Almost every time."

2. THERE'S A GOOD WAY AND THERE'S A BEST WAY

There's a common belief among therapists who work with marriage and family relationships that, as one marriage leader told me, "It doesn't really matter exactly what you do as long as you start a purposeful effort to do *something* positive. Many programs work, and the level of efficacy is a function of the amount of time devoted to the change process."

Respectfully, based on my survey results, I disagree. There's a way of using the kindness tool that makes a reasonable difference, and there's a way that makes a *big* difference. Although it is true that "just doing something" is crucial if it wakes us up from default patterns and gets us into better ones, I've found that many people are already doing something. For example, as mentioned in chapter 3, they are trying hard but aren't seeing enough results because they are trying hard in the wrong areas—or in good areas that simply aren't the best ones.

But a daily effort toward each of the three areas of kindness (say nothing negative, practice praise, and do a small act of kindness) is one best practice that makes a measurable difference in the outcome of relationships. You see, most people who take the 30-Day Kindness Challenge elect on our website to receive a daily reminder e-mail with a tip of the day as an optional idea to get the creative juices flowing. (For example, an act of kindness hint might be, "Think of a chore that your person dislikes—unloading the dishwasher, changing the toner for the printer at the office, cleaning up the gym at the end of recess—and do it for them today.") We've found that some people tend to focus primarily on the tip of the day, while others focus primarily on the three elements of the Challenge, whether or not they do the tips.

Our survey results were dramatically different between those two groups. Among those who focused on the tips—and thus were essentially being purposeful about doing or saying something kind each day—there was a good level of improvement. But among those who actually practiced the three elements of the 30-Day Kindness Challenge, even without the tip, the improvement was dramatic. As just one example, among those in less-than-perfect romantic relationships, if they focused primarily on the tip of the day, 55 percent of those relationships improved. Among those who did the actual Challenge, it was 74 percent—that's 19 points higher!

And this was a typical result. We commonly saw a fifteen- to twenty-point swing (or more) between the two groups on all sorts of measures: they were far more likely to be happy, feel appreciated, even see improvement in their sex life if they did the actual Challenge, whether or not they used the tips. Another way of putting it is this: participants improve their likelihood of good results by one-third or more if they practice the three Challenge elements instead of only the daily tips.

Now, just to be clear: if focusing on the daily tips is what gets you started, energized, and motivated to continue, there's nothing wrong with doing the 30-Day Kindness Challenge that way! If that works for you, by all means do it! Many men, in particular, felt like they could more successfully start with the daily tips and try to focus on the three kindness elements as they went. Make the decision that will be most effective for *you*. And whether or not you focus on the tips or simply use them as daily reminder e-mails, you can sign up for the 30-Day Kindness Challenge at JoinTheKindnessChallenge.com. (You can also see several sets of daily tips in the Toolbox section.)

3. What You Put in Is What Will Come Out

It's a commonly accepted truth: what you listen to with your ears is going to come out of your mouth. Or if you read books filled with cutting satire, you'll probably be more sarcastic, simply because that seems normal and acceptable and is in the front of your mind. Conversely, if you listen to podcasts filled with inspiration, you'll probably be more optimistic and encouraging in your speech.

While I did this research, I heard again and again that people who watched contentious political commentary on the news found themselves getting contentious. As one man put it, "I actually had to stop watching some of that stuff. I found myself getting all agitated and defensive with my family and friends, and I couldn't figure out why. Then I realized: everything I'm watching is agitated and defensive!"

Thankfully, changing what you put in changes what comes out. One longtime friend of ours has always embraced extremely partisan Republican beliefs. So partisan, in fact, that although he is reasonable in every other area of life and business, I found it unpleasant and uncomfortable to talk to him about politics because he so strongly and viscerally disliked anything to do with Democrats. Although I lean conservative, I've worked for and taken positions on both sides of the aisle, and I am deeply troubled by how divided our country has become. So for years I didn't talk to him about politics.

Not long ago, though, Jeff and I caught up with him over coffee. As I described the theme of *The Kindness Challenge,* he told us, "This is needed. We need more civility in our country. I feel like we're going backward. And I feel like I am. You probably hadn't heard about this, but last year I realized I was too politically negative about the other side. I felt I had to be kinder in my heart to them. So I decided to take some measures to do that."

Fascinated, I asked him, "What did you do?"

"I took lessons in how to be a good Democrat."

"You *what*?"

He smiled slightly. "I took lessons in how to be a good Democrat. I went to a series of meetings put on by the Democratic Party to help their folks understand how to influence legislation and so on. I went to listen and try to understand their perspective." He smiled ruefully. "It's not a total success story. It didn't have a huge impact on my view of the world. But I have realized it made me much less strident regarding whomever I was relating to."

Since that coffee Jeff and I have seen him many times, and even though we are in a presidential election season as I write these words and politics has come up many times, I have not once heard our friend mention a negative word about those with whom he strongly disagrees. He will very clearly state his disagreement with various positions and policies but is living the adage that you can disagree without being disagreeable. Since his goal was to be less negative and more kind, I'd say that is a huge success story!

4. What You Focus On Is What You Will See

A cousin principle covers not the external (what you say) but the internal (what you see). What you allow yourself to focus on will impact what you actually observe around you: you will notice more and more of what you focus on or, conversely, less and less of what you don't want to see.

The beauty of this aspect of the kindness tool is that *it provides its own motivation for using it*! If you want to improve your relationship with someone, focus on those things you already like and appreciate about them. You'll find yourself seeing those things much more, which will make you want to be kind as a result.

And unfortunately, the reverse is also true.

I have studied divorce for many years in many ways, both up close with friends going through it and at arm's length as a researcher. And I've noticed that where the divorce is particularly contentious, one or both parties have generally become convinced that their spouse has some sort of personality disorder or other psychological/emotional issue ("Oh, he's definitely a sociopath! Here's what he did the other day . . .").

Now, perhaps all those contentious divorces did occur because one partner had a psychological problem. But statistically, I doubt it. I interviewed a long-time specialized divorce lawyer about this, and he said,

> I usually represent the party who *doesn't* want the divorce. Among their
> spouses, well north of 90 percent put forward some sort of argument
> that my client has a psychological issue, because they are trying to justify
> the divorce to themselves or trying to get primary custody of the kids.
> Borderline personality disorder is one that I see argued pretty often. Of
> course, the real percentage of BPD in society is tiny, but these folks have
> come to be so angry with their husband or wife that all they can see is
> negative, erratic behavior. And if they allow themselves to reflect on the
> good in their spouse, they won't feel as justified in the divorce. So it is
> common at this stage to see this. It's very sad.
>
> What is interesting is that I've also seen some couples reconcile, even
> at this stage. I'm always watching for that opportunity, since I do talk to
> so many people who regret the divorce years later. But the main thing

that leads to reconciliation is when one person's perspective changes. It is very unusual that the situation itself changes; it is more of a matter of what they are willing to see. And once they are willing to see the good things, they start to focus on those more, so the situation seems more balanced and hopeful.

5. What You Think Is What You Will Say

Did you know people can hear you thinking? How, you ask? It's because what you allow yourself to think in your head will eventually come out of your mouth. Think on good things, and what will come out will generally be kind and good. Think on what is frustrating, annoying, or irritating, and I guarantee that will come out too.

We saw this in an amusing way in our own home. One weekend Jeff was out taking one of his regular hikes on the Appalachian Trail and I'd allowed our then-fourteen-year-old daughter to sleep in his place. We both were exhausted, so she fell asleep pretty quickly and I read a book on my tablet for about fifteen minutes before switching off the power. The moment the electronic glow shut off, I heard from beside me, in the huffiest and most disrespectful of teenage voices, "Finally! You stopped reading and turned off that light so I can go to sleep!"

Shocked (since the tone of voice made it clear she was not joking), I turned toward her . . . and saw she was actually asleep. She was talking in her sleep! That made a lot more sense, because she would never have used that extreme tone if she were conscious. (Well . . . almost never.)

The next day when I asked her, she had no memory of it. Then she looked at me as if trying to decide whether to share something or not. She finally said, "Um . . . I would never say that to you out loud, but I do say that stuff in my head sometimes. I guess it came out."

It works the same way with each of us. If we allow ourselves to think huffy, irritable, and unkind thoughts, they will make their way out of our mouths.

6. What You Say and Do Is What You Will Feel

As implied by what we have discussed thus far, what you say and do actually shapes what you feel. In other words, when you act kind, respectful, loving, and positive, you begin to *want* to be kind, respectful, loving, and positive, which is one of the key reasons the Kindness Challenge works so well to improve difficult relationships.

Now, I realize it might be easy to dismiss the idea of systematic kindness and positivity as naive and impractical. For example, I used to use the phrase "I don't want to be Pollyanna-ish" to essentially roll my eyes at unrealistic levels of optimism. And then I actually read Eleanor H. Porter's book *Pollyanna*. The story is about a young girl who transforms her world by refusing to be negative—even when her circumstances are—and by being glad instead. Her missionary father modeled that outlook on life even though he lacked many material things. He took to heart the biblical command to find ways to rejoice in all things, even those things that are difficult.

I realized that sounded kind of familiar.

In the letter the apostle Paul wrote to the church in the ancient city of Philippi, he pleaded with two church leaders to resolve what was apparently a serious and well-known disagreement or personality conflict. He challenged them, "Always be full of joy in the Lord" and "considerate in all you do." And then he told them (and us!) how to accomplish those two outcomes: by praying and thanking God instead of worrying and by resolutely focusing on the positive. As Paul said in his conclusion, "Fix your thoughts on what is true, and honorable, and right, and pure, and lovely, and admirable. Think about things that are excellent and worthy of praise."[1]

As noted in chapter 1, if you fix your thoughts and words on what is *not* right, on what is irritating you, you'll be more irritated and more irritable. But if you refuse to do that and fix your thoughts on what *is* right instead, you'll be far more glad—and far more kind.

Being Pollyanna-ish, it turns out, is a choice to look at the world through kind-colored glasses. And it is a great prescription for how to improve our feelings about a situation.

7. KINDNESS IS CATCHING: IF YOU ARE KIND, THEY'LL BE KIND TOO

For years scientists have known that smiling is contagious: if you smile at someone, they smile back. Not long ago they discovered at least one probable cause, a phenomenon in the brain called mirror neurons. These little babies seem to give you automatic subconscious empathy and association with, for example, the friend who is grinning at you as she describes her child's antics, the homeless person looking with awe at the plate of food you're serving him, or the person who begins to get emotional as she talks about losing someone dear to her.[2] One result of this neurology: the way we treat others tends to trigger the way they treat us. If we scowl, they scowl back.

In 2009 the government of France was reeling from a 17 percent drop in tourism in just one year. Surveys by the travel firm TripAdvisor had long found that Paris visitors viewed residents as hostile and unfriendly. And suddenly, with the worry and stress of the global recession, tourists wanted to go to friendlier shores. So the French government acted in a way consistent with sound neuroscience: they hired people to smile at others on street corners.[3]

I'm not kidding.

They hoped these "smile ambassadors" would begin to reverse the trend and help draw in more tourists, but unfortunately they were like a few drops in a very big bucket. To effect bigger change, the government pleaded with residents for the sake of the national economy (of which tourism is a huge part) to at least be polite and kind to nonresidents. There were signs the message was being heeded; in 2013 Paris moved up to TripAdvisor's number one "Traveler's Choice Destination."[4] Only time will tell whether the kindness effort will spread. But if they focus on it, it should. Because kindness is catching.

8. Practice Makes Perfect: Kindness Must Be a Habit to Become a Lifestyle

Being kind consistently has to become a habit. If it doesn't, we are all but certain to slip back to our old defaults—see principle 1—and inertia will take over. To build a habit, repetition over time is one of the things that matters most. (Sad news for those who have asked me, "Um, do you have a two-day Kindness Challenge?") But once it does become a habit, you'll see opportunities for kindness everywhere.

Last Fourth of July, our family was at the annual country fair in the rural area where my parents have lived since they retired. It is a popular affair with games, music, food booths, huge inflatable slides and obstacle courses, and of course spectacular fireworks after dark. I was standing in line with my then-twelve-year-old son, waiting for him to go up the massive Cliff Hanger slide, when we heard a terrified sobbing from the very top. A little four-year-old girl had climbed up and was stuck; she was too scared to slide down. After unsuccessful attempts to persuade her, her father made the awkward (for an adult) climb to the summit, with the crowd of at least forty people silent and watching below. Suddenly the woman next to me blurted out, "I think this must be the cutest thing I've ever seen." She turned to all the people around her. "When he comes down, y'all better clap! I hope everyone claps for this man!"

Up above us, the dad gathered his tearful little girl into his arms, and with her face buried in her daddy's shoulder and her arms around his neck, he gingerly began crabbing back down the almost-vertical staircase with her clinging to him like a front backpack. And with one voice, the crowd below started clapping and cheering. The dad was startled, then started grinning. You could tell the accolades made his day.

When the commotion died down, I asked the woman beside me, "Is he your husband?"

"No, no," she said with a laugh. "I just try to make it a habit to encourage people, you know? It has to be a habit. Otherwise it doesn't happen."

It has to be a habit. Otherwise it doesn't happen. True that. I had stood there at the base of the slide with thirty-nine others and only *one* of us brought up what should have been in the minds of all—but wasn't.

Thankfully, if you *do* repeat kindness, a new habit is easily built because the rewards are so great. Most people prefer a life marked by kindness. So build a habit. Then build a lifestyle.

The problem is that many of us have *already* built all sorts of habits that we don't even know we have. And without our realizing it, a host of them aren't kind! Or they are interfering with our ability to be kind. As we'll see in the next chapter, we do have to have our eyes opened to all those unseen bad habits before we can truly become people whose lives are marked by the good ones.

Think You Know How to Be Kind? Think Again

No More Kindness Blindness

Most of us think we are already kind—that we use the tool of kindness pretty frequently, thank you very much. At the very least, we certainly don't think of ourselves as *un*kind.

Yet in my research I discovered we are usually a bit deluded! We're not nearly as kind as we think we are. It's like my tendency to say, "I got the car's oil changed just three or four months ago," and then I check and discover that, uh, nope, it's been a year!

This particular delusion is exactly what we discovered as we started surveying participants in the Kindness Challenge. It was a bit amusing. Before they started the Challenge, our participants would look at a given survey question and say (for example), "Oh, sure, I express appreciation to my spouse a lot. More than once a day." Once they actually started the Challenge they would realize, *Holy cow, no I don't! I am actually expressing appreciation only two or three times a week!* So then participants would work hard to state appreciation more regularly, and at the end of the thirty days would finally end up in reality where they thought they had started in theory.

But just as profound as their shift in action was the reason for it: the vast majority of the group was suddenly more *aware*.

Eyes Opened

Did you become more aware of things you were doing / not doing that negatively impacted your partner that you didn't realize before?

Yes, it made me more aware.	95%
No, my awareness didn't change.	0%
This doesn't apply, because I was already very aware of what I was doing/not doing in the relationship.	5%

Thankfully, once the blindness drops from our eyes and we learn a few specifics—exactly what we'll be covering in the next few chapters—a whole new world of opportunity opens up to us. Suddenly we see our real competence at kindness, or lack thereof. We know how to avoid various unkind words and actions that we didn't even know we were doing before. And we know what actions will most improve our relationships.

Now, to be sure, people often feel *consciously* blind too. I have talked to many a confused parent, spouse, or business leader who is looking for solutions because they recognize that a relationship is in trouble and that they are not giving their child, partner, or employee what that person needs. And those individuals are actually in a better starting place in some ways because they recognize their blindness. They're very aware that they don't know how to be kind in the way that will make the most difference.

The rest of us have to get there. So before we can dive into what each of us most needs to work on, we have to look at two common blind spots that will prevent us from being kind if we aren't aware of them. Just as we check our blind spots while driving a car on the highway, we can learn to check our actions for both of these.

Check Your Blind Spots

Blind Spot #1: We're More Negative Than We Think We Are

One woman told me of a time she had done something similar to the 30-Day Kindness Challenge on her own. Although she described herself as a pretty easygoing person, she had been irritated for two years with a colleague named Phillip. His data analysis was central to her work, but his thorough approach led to both an exasperating degree of slowness and spreadsheets she found difficult to read. Her irritation had turned into a personality conflict, which turned into departmental drama, which turned into a situation in which both their jobs were seriously at risk. Their boss said he didn't want to hear one negative word, sigh of exasperation, or implication of negativity from either of them about the other for one month. If he did, they should consider dismissal highly likely.

"I didn't think it would be difficult," she told me, "mostly because I didn't think I was really all that negative. Until I was suddenly focused on the need to keep my job. If you had asked me before, I would have said I expressed some form of negative comment about Phillip twice a week. But once I was super-aware of my boss watching, I realized it was more like twice a *day*. In previous months, a colleague would ask, 'Have you sent in your daily projections?' and I would roll my eyes or use this slightly sarcastic tone, like, 'I will just as soon as Mr. Slowpoke gets me his numbers.' Suddenly I couldn't do that anymore. I had to politely say, 'I'll send it as soon as I get Phil's numbers.' It was eyeopening. And a little disturbing."

I was fascinated. "Did you make it the whole month?"

"Yep, both of us did." She gave me a ghost of a smile. "And it changed things pretty dramatically. We'll never be let's-get-coffee buddies, but we actually like working with each other now. Once we started forcing ourselves *not* to be negative, those issues just didn't loom as large. I began to actually appreciate how thorough his analyses were, and he realized that my Type A approach was what kept us hitting our sales targets. He even put a few summary tabs on his spreadsheet because he saw the reason for it, instead of seeing it as criticism of his data. When it comes to work stuff, I do see him as a real asset now."

Her comments describe a classic blind spot. She didn't know what she didn't know—in her case, how often she was thinking and doing something negative interpersonally that actively sabotaged her productivity, her peace of mind (and everyone else's!), and her relationship with her coworker. In the research, we've seen this type of pattern often.

As you'll see in the coming chapters, even those of us who already care about being kind and positive have no idea just how often we are *un*kind, negative, unengaged, or distracted. Also, there are times we may in fact be somewhat positive and appreciative—just not nearly as much as we think we are. Or we simply have no idea how often we are missing opportunities to be caring, loving, engaged, or fully attuned to the other person.

Bottom line: whether or not we are already focused on the need for kindness, most of us have no idea how much we're missing. And often those elements that we're missing are some of the most important.

Blind Spot #2: We're Blind to How the Other Person Feels

We often simply don't recognize (and don't recognize that we don't recognize!) what is going on inside the other person, his or her point of view, or how we can respond in a healthy, productive, kind way.

Early in my research process, a wonderful pastor-and-wife counseling team offered their large multicultural church in North Carolina to serve as our first official test site for the 30-Day Kindness Challenge. I flew in to conduct some interviews during a period when some people had finished the Challenge, some were just starting, and others were right in the middle. One interview was with a woman named Amanda who was two weeks into doing the Challenge for her husband of seventeen years and whose eyes had just recently begun to open in a big way.

We talked for a few minutes about the serious challenges in their marriage resulting from the stress of difficult finances (including her previous job loss, which precipitated losing their house) and a recent bout of depression brought on by her daughter (from a previous marriage) going off to college. Their current marital conflict centered on her daughter's need for help with tuition and replacing a totaled car. Amanda wanted to give her daughter some money for the car right away, but her husband strongly disagreed and wanted to set stringent conditions.

I asked if Amanda had seen any changes—good or bad—in the two weeks of doing the 30-Day Kindness Challenge. She nodded. "I *do* see a change in my husband. I see a change in myself. Before the Kindness Challenge, honestly, I would have done whatever I wanted for my daughter and not worried about how he felt about it. But I have started to listen more when he says, 'These are *our* finances, and we need to be in agreement.'"

I asked, "Why is doing the Challenge leading you to listen to him more?"

"Because I have had to find things about him to praise, so I praised him for providing and for being careful about money. And that meant I had to see that he's pretty rational about it—whether I want to admit it or not! It's like I have to put myself in his shoes."

So being intentional about what she was doing and saying made her more aware of what he was thinking?

"Oh yes! Ordinarily I wouldn't think about that. Like with my daughter. She's coming home tomorrow and I have to face both of them. I have to think, *Are we buying her a car?*"

As she spoke, Amanda started to get visibly agitated. "And suddenly what is weighing on my mind is, *How is he going to feel about it?* and *How is he going to view me and how I value him?*"

Her voice rose a bit. "So if I were to go and buy this car, what would it say to him? That I completely disrespect him? Oh my gosh, I wouldn't even have been *thinking* about that if I hadn't been looking at this for the last two weeks! Holy cow, I'm having my own little therapy session here as I'm talking myself through this!"

I forced myself to keep a straight face and asked whether she was seeing his feelings and point of view on other issues beyond finances. She said, "Yeah. I have this emotional attachment to my daughter, sometimes at his expense. But now that I'm more aware of what he's thinking, I'm sure he's felt unwanted or unneeded because my attachment to her pulled me away from him. When she went off to college, I felt like my life was ending. So I realize now that my focus wasn't on my husband at all, even though I needed him so much."

Amanda started to get agitated again, and she put both hands to her head. "Oh my gosh, he must have felt terrible! And I recognize that in the grand scheme of things, my daughter is going to have her own life, but I will have to live with what we decide in the next few weeks for the marriage for the rest of our life. And I've never done that. I've never put my husband's feelings first before!"

It's Not You, It's Me

All of us probably need to have our eyes opened. All of us need to figure out how to better implement kindness in our relationships. And there are two different ways of doing that—one that has an even bigger impact than the other.

First is awareness. Not of what the other person should be doing, but of our own kindness blindness and what *we* need to be doing. Reading this book is one example of how to get there: We learn, and we think about how to apply what we learn. We read things that open our eyes in various ways. We are struck by something we hear on the radio. We listen to our spouse, friend, or colleague explain how they think, and suddenly we understand something we didn't before. All those things will help shake us out of our blind spots, especially about our lack of knowledge.

The second is action. We will never fully see what kindnesses we aren't doing until we actually try it. And trying it doesn't mean a vague approach like "I'll be nicer to people." It means doing something very specific, something like the 30-Day Kindness Challenge to tackle the three elements of kindness, or a similar initiative.

So let's tackle how to do each of the three elements of kindness, one by one, in the next three chapters.

Part II

Let's Do This: Thirty Days to a

Kinder You

The 30-Day Kindness Challenge

Element #1: Nix the Negatives

Say nothing negative, either to your person or about them to someone else. (If negative feedback is unavoidable, be constructive or encouraging without a negative tone.)

Element #2: Practice Praise

Every day, find one positive thing that you can sincerely praise or affirm about your person and tell them, and tell someone else.

Element #3: Carry Out Kindness

Every day, do a small act of kindness or generosity for your person.

For husbands doing the 30-Day Kindness Challenge for
their wives, see chapter 9 for an alternative Element #1.

Nix the Negatives

Seven Types of Negativity You Didn't Know You Had

> *Element #1* Say nothing negative, either to your person or about them to someone else.

When you think about the relationship you are trying to improve, how often do you say or imply anything negative to or about the other person? Or if you are focusing on the practice of kindness more broadly, rather than with one specific person, how often do you verbalize negative thoughts in general?

Most of us would never think of ourselves as negative, and yet when we are frustrated, irritated, hurt, or angry, negative words and thoughts are often an unrecognized default. For example, do you sigh in exasperation when your son forgets his homework or the grocery store checker is slow? Make it clear with a look that you are disappointed in your spouse? Vent about your biology class lab partner being late again?

Once we start paying attention, we realize (to our chagrin!) that we slip into those patterns easily. And stopping them can take more work than we thought. One woman started the 30-Day Kindness Challenge on a Monday morning, thinking it would be fairly easy, and by Tuesday afternoon she found herself screaming at her bewildered husband, "I'm trying to do the Kindness Challenge, but you're making it so hard!"

Remember Nadia's story of her refusing-to-vent-about-the-boss colleague in chapter 1? As her colleague said, negativity may be easy—but it changes us. For example, despite the momentary gratification of venting or getting something off our chest, the ultimate change in how we feel is not for the better. I've seen this truth for years in my own research and more comprehensively in many other studies.

One classic study found just how easy it is even for *simulated* negative words and actions to lead to very real negative feelings and behavior. In 1971 Stanford University psychology professor Dr. Philip G. Zimbardo and a team of researchers decided to study the effects of incarceration on prisoners and guards. Mentally and physically normal, healthy young men were randomly chosen to be either prisoners or guards in a Stanford basement wing modified to look like a prison. Intended to last two weeks, the study had to be discontinued after six days. The words and behavior the guards used to control the prisoners so thoroughly altered their feelings about the prisoners and their own authority that they became aggressive and even sadistic, and the prisoners were being seriously mistreated.[1]

As one psychiatrist told me, "The Zimbardo prison study at Stanford is a powerful testimony to how emotions often follow behaviors. Once the students started acting the part of prison guards, they began to feel the part. People assume that emotions are what shape behavior, but this is not necessarily true. The relationship is reciprocal; behavior often shapes how we feel about things. This is a well-documented finding."

Thankfully the truth that behavior shapes feelings doesn't apply only to negative feelings. The good news is that stopping negativity in its tracks and building positivity and kindness changes us as well.

THE PROMISE OF POSITIVITY

You will find that as you gain the new habit of nixing the negativity, something remarkable happens. You will have a lighter heart, greater peace, and much more enjoyment of your life and relationships, and you will see more constructive and powerful outcomes of your efforts in the world.

How can I say that? Those were the consistent, documented results among most of those who did the Kindness Challenge for just a few weeks—not to mention those for whom this became (or already was) a lifestyle.

For example, among those with room for improvement in their relationship with a spouse and who did the actual Challenge for at least two weeks, 67 percent reported that enjoyment in their relationship improved, with 72 percent of that group declaring they were now happy in their marriages! (When looking at the total group, including those who didn't have room for improvement because they were already so happy, the overall percentage of those who said they were happy rose to 82 percent.)

More Kindness, More Happiness

What happened when those with room for improvement in their marriage did the 30-Day Kindness Challenge?

	Before	After
Percent of spouses who said their enjoyment of the relationship improved:	67%	
Percent of spouses who said they were happy in marriage:	37%	72%

Note: Among those who had room for improvement in enjoyment of their relationship.

Even more compelling, brain science backs this up. Neuroscience research has demonstrated conclusively that the choice to limit negativity and increase positivity has a clinically measurable impact on how we feel.

In 2008 United Kingdom researchers investigated a pattern noticed by plastic surgeons who had used Botox on their clients to reduce facial lines and wrinkles. After treatment, patients routinely reported feeling fewer negative feelings and more positive ones—enough that some doctors suggested Botox might become a treatment for depression! But why did it work that way? Well, Botox injections reduce frown lines by temporarily paralyzing the facial muscles that cause them. The study found that when patients were unable to frown or crease their foreheads to show negativity or displeasure, they actually experienced *far fewer of those negative emotions.*

As the researchers put it, "The results support the facial feedback view that frowning can make one unhappier. Treatments that prevent frowning correlate with reduced negative mood."[2] And the newly positive feelings didn't come about simply because the patients felt more attractive, either. There was no statistically significant correlation. The researchers concluded,

> Those [in the study] who had received BTX-A [Botox] treatment to the forehead had a significantly more positive mood than those who had not, and this was carried mainly by lower anxiety and depression scores. . . .
>
> The paralysis of the corrugator [frown] muscles, which makes it impossible to make many negative facial expression[s], causes negative moods to be harder to maintain: The lack of the negative mood feedback from the facial muscles leads these people to feel happier.[3]

Moral of the story? You can skip the shot of Botox to the forehead and accomplish the same emotional outcome simply by refusing to express negativity—whether in words, facial expressions, or body language.

We're Not Venting, We're Building Up Steam

But, you may ask, isn't it important sometimes to express negative emotions when they occur to prevent worse ones down the road? Shouldn't we be allowed to express anger, for example? In fact, if you're angry or frustrated, isn't it better to let a little steam out of the kettle now in order to avoid boiling over or exploding later? That's the whole point of venting, right?

First, certainly we are allowed to express anger. Especially in a relationship that matters deeply, we need to be able to share how we feel. But remember, this is the *Kindness* Challenge. We are trying to stop all negativity for a period of time. And if something negative must be expressed, it doesn't have to be done negatively; we can communicate serious concerns without a negative tone and with as much grace as possible.

My friend Lysa TerKeurst's best-selling book *Unglued* unpacks how to handle various negative emotions in a healthy way. She summarized a few practical suggestions for me:

> I always say that our feelings are indicators, not dictators. Negative feelings indicate that an issue needs to be addressed but should never dictate that we address it in a negative manner. Start with a three-second pause. Patience is a choice, and I'm capable of being patient by choice even if patience isn't my natural inclination. That also allows the Holy Spirit time to interrupt what might be my more natural response! Then in that pause I remember to attack the issues, not the people involved. Finally, I ask myself, "What's my real desire? Do I want to prove that I'm right or improve this relationship?" I always have to remember *I can't do both at the same time.*[4]

Second, and more critical, the old idea that it's better to "let the steam out of the kettle" turns out to be completely inaccurate neurologically! Researchers like Dr. Brad Bushman at Ohio State University have been studying anger processing for years. These researchers have discovered that expressing anger actually further activates an interconnected anger system in the brain and thus is like choosing to turn up the heat. So as you vent, the steam only builds. (We need to stop thinking of it as *venting* and think of it as *building up steam* instead!) They've discovered that a better analogy is this: if a pot of water is boiling, we can put the lid on tight and remove it from the heat. Our determined choice to be calm is like a lid that smothers the steam, and when we remove or distract ourselves from whatever is stoking the flame, we find our anger cooling off until, in many cases, we're simply not angry anymore.[5]

Nineteenth-century psychologist, philosopher, and physician William James articulated this truth long before modern neuroscience proved it: "Refuse to express a passion, and it dies. . . . If we wish to conquer undesirable emotional tendencies in ourselves, we must assiduously, and in the first instance cold-bloodedly, go through the *outward motions* of those contrary dispositions we prefer to cultivate."[6]

Modern parlance? Fake it until you feel it. And it works. For thirty days, at least, refuse to express any negative feelings about the person and relationship you're trying to improve, no matter how justified.

Eliminating negativity is the first element of kindness and the first step in the Kindness Challenge. It is also the highest-leverage action. Without it, you will find it is too easy to sabotage all your other efforts, preventing your good actions on the outside from changing your feelings on the inside. But with it, you will find yourself *wanting* to change.

IF YOU DON'T HAVE ANYTHING NICE TO SAY . . .

So in what ways do you tend to be negative and unkind? As imperfect human beings, all of us have something we need to address, even if we've never thought of it as negativity before. Before I started this book, I would have sworn that I was rarely negative—until I began the research in depth and started cataloging all the different types of negativity and ways it can play out. And I saw, *Oh my goodness, I do that . . .* and *that . . .* and *that. . . .*

As Sarah took the 30-Day Kindness Challenge, she discovered that her main expression of negativity was discussing her mom with her husband. Her mom, Marianne, is a difficult, easily offended person who lives with the family because she has a lot of health issues—like the mother-in-law I described in chapter 2. Sarah has a lot of anger and resentment because she feels her mom is taking advantage of them. Marianne is still fairly young, her disabilities are directly tied to various life choices, and Sarah feels her mother hasn't taken responsibility for either keeping up her health or taking steps to get disability-related help.

Sarah explained, "I have young kids, a full-time job, and honestly, I really shouldn't have to be caring for my mother at this point. We especially don't want her hair-trigger way of handling things to spread to our kids. It has been really hard. But we don't have a choice right now, so I wanted to at least figure out how to have a better relationship."

While doing the 30-Day Kindness Challenge, she identified several ways her thoughts, words, and actions about and toward her mom had been negative. In particular, she realized, "My husband and I had gotten into a rut of unproductive complaining to each other about her." As she put it,

> I would vent to my husband, but eventually I wondered, *What is at the heart of the venting? Am I venting to be mean and because I'm frustrated with her? Or because I want to help and figure out what do we do with this?*
>
> Not long before the Kindness Challenge started, my mom and I got in this big argument. Usually I don't address issues with my mom, because if I do she spits out fire. But this one day I needed to raise something, and she said some ugly things that really, really hurt me. I was telling my husband about it later and got mad all over again. My heart was beating fast and my hands were shaking and I said, "I can't talk about this anymore because it's not helping. It's taking me back to the place I was during the actual fight!"
>
> Although talking to my husband is important for my state of mind, this was a purely negative replay just for the sake of telling him, rather than telling him to try to get somewhere with it. So it *wasn't*

constructive for my state of mind! In fact, it was hurtful because I made myself go back to thinking about it, and I got worked up again about something that was already over.

Once the thirty days ended, Sarah told us it had made a great deal of difference in how she felt about her mom and the situation. "Nixing the negativity made me have compassion instead of anger. It's fascinating, actually: when you aren't allowed to be negative, you talk about things in such a way that you don't *let* yourself go back to that place of anger. In fact, I find myself being more understanding. When I don't let myself be negative, I am more likely to care and to try to see where the other person is coming from. And that actually takes the place of the anger."

> **Question to Consider**
>
> When I vent, what is the heart behind it? Do I want to get something off my chest and feel better by complaining? Or do I want to figure out a constructive solution?

Sarah realized her mom had had a pretty traumatic past and childhood. So she had lots of emotional baggage and dealt with things differently from the way Sarah and her husband would like her to.

That is hard on us, but I really do understand why she is as she is. And yes, I need to be able to talk with my husband about things that I can't discuss with anyone else. But if it is always "Oh, this is really frustrating!" it isn't getting us anywhere. But if we can talk about what to do to make the situation better, even if realistically it is not likely to happen, it changes the dynamic.

For example, yesterday I was at work, my husband was home, and my mom was bent out of shape and showing him these text messages from her brothers. My husband would say, "I don't see how you're pulling that out of what he said." Later, instead of saying, "Oh my gosh, she is so annoying," he told me, "You know, your mom needs counseling. I really think that would help. Do you think she would go if we paid for it?" She may never take the offer, but just the fact that we were talking about her in that way, instead of complaining with no resolution, was huge.

We found that not being negative prompted us to *think* kindly, not just speak more kindly. When you're saying or thinking something negative—even if you hadn't really seen it that way—it changes your soul for the worse. It's like being a teenager who runs around with a bad crowd. But when you practice eliminating negativity, it is like being around people who change you for the better.

What Is Your Negativity Pattern?

All of us have to identify our individual negativity patterns—the ways in which we tend to be negative or at least aren't already being positive—in order to confront the unkind behaviors and replace them with healthy ones.

For the rest of this chapter, I'll outline seven types of negativity in thought, word, or action—including many things we may have never seen as damaging before. And I'll share what happens in our lives and relationships when we eliminate them. Take a look at the lists in the following pages to see if you recognize any patterns. In particular, as you think about a person with whom you have some strife, anger, or past hurt (your spouse, boss, mother-in-law) or a group of people you tend to be at odds with (people who drive too fast, members of the other political party, your school administrators), which of the listed words or actions are relatively common reactions on your part?

Keep in mind that everyone will experience these reactions occasionally. What we want is to identify your *patterns*. So check off or write down the items that apply with some regularity, especially with that person or group you identified. Also, since these are general lists intended primarily to jog your memory, fill in the blanks or write notes with more specifics as needed. Include examples. "Getting exasperated with Mom when she calls" is a more specific and memorable way of capturing and understanding what you need to change than the simple word "Irritation." (This exercise will also help you later when you go back and map your main issues on the simple, personalized Self-Assessment Action Plan or the other assessments at JoinTheKindnessChallenge.com.)

Once you know how you tend to be negative, you'll be better able to work on nixing it—and see the benefits of doing so!

1. "This Will Be Hard"

The very first negative many of us have to confront is simply the knee-jerk reaction that "saying nothing negative is going to be *hard*." A few years ago, I was speaking on relationships at a women's conference. I suggested that the women do the Challenge for a husband, boyfriend, or other relationship as their next step after the conference. When I said, "There are three steps," the women all looked very interested and I could see many prepare to take notes. But when I said, "Step 1: say nothing negative about your husband or boyfriend—either to him or about him to somebody else," a surprisingly intense reaction swept the room. Groans and whispers broke out everywhere as the women either processed how often they really did say negative things or doubted their ability to avoid it for thirty days.

When I began studying kindness, I realized that many of us have bought into a lie that it is extremely difficult to change how we think and speak. But in most cases, unless there is something unusually intense and systemic impacting the relationship (for example, a serious betrayal or addiction), this isn't the case. Instead, confronting negativity requires (as we've said) being very purposeful. It requires being attuned to something you didn't think about before and acting with self-discipline instead of letting your default tendency take over.

Reversing negativity isn't particularly natural for any of us. It requires attention and care. Yes, it can be a challenge because it can be immensely frustrating to force ourselves to stop what is about to come out of our mouths when we really want to let it rip instead! But in most cases, none of that is necessarily complicated, painful, or ultradifficult to do.

My friend Emerson Eggerichs, the best-selling author of *Love and Respect,* gave me a great perspective on this recently:

> A lot of women come up to me when their marriages are in crisis, and they think my solution is going to be some ten-step plan. I say, "Got a pencil? Do three things: Number one: be friendly. Number two: be friendly. Number three: be friendly." It sounds so simple, but it is revolutionary. We heard from one man whose wife did this, and after ten days he said, "Give it to me straight. The doctor told you I was going to die, didn't he?"
>
> So often what is needed is simply stopping negativity. There's always plenty of positive there along with the negative. So once they look for it, they find it. Then they come back and say, "Thanks for having me do that; I fell in love all over again."[7]

To be candid, reversing negativity is primarily a matter of reexamining our priorities. We have a default assumption that other things (for example, feeling good by getting my anger off my chest) are the greatest good even if they damage the relationship, our attitudes, or our state of mind. Yet in most cases, if we were to sit down and evaluate the situation dispassionately, we would rarely or never agree that the damage was worth it. So we have to recognize negative words or body language before they come out and choose to respond in a different way. It doesn't have to be hard; it does have to be purposeful.

☺ **When we nix that negative, everything seems easier and more doable.** Instead of saying, "This is hard," think and say, "I need to think before I speak, but I can do it." When you do, you'll find that everything seems easier. You've stopped mentally sabotaging everything you need to work on. And you've given yourself a very real boost to your ability to do it.

2. Exasperation, Irritation, and Pointing Out Mistakes

Can I sheepishly admit this is my biggest negativity problem? I don't generally talk or vent about people to others. And avoiding some of the other negatives isn't a huge issue for me. But I can heave an exasperated sigh with the best of them. I use an angry tone of voice far too often. My kids are the most common targets of this delightful habit ("I told you to pick that up!" "What on earth were you doing the last ten minutes when you should have been getting ready?") but are by no means the only ones.

A few years ago I had called a large financial services company for help reversing a simple but sizable error on a bill. I tried to hold on to my patience for an hour as I was transferred from one department to the next, placed on hold, asked to repeat myself over and over, and disconnected twice. By the time I reached the right department, let's just say I wasn't hiding my exasperation. I apologized to the final representative about it and explained that I was at the end of my rope. She was extraordinarily polite as she asked the same questions the other reps had asked and I gave clipped, frustrated answers. Finally, the bill was corrected and she asked the usual parting question: "Mrs. Feldhahn, is the issue resolved to your satisfaction?" When I said it was, she said, "Thank you for allowing us to serve you. And oh, by the way, I loved your book."

How's that for a punch in the gut? As you can imagine, I felt an incredible sense of conviction. I was almost shaking. I became uncomfortably aware of just how frustrated I had sounded throughout my exchanges with the last few customer service representatives—reps who may or may not have been doing their jobs properly, mind you, but who deserved my respect as people. And not just to preserve my reputation as an author but because God has asked me to show love to everyone around me and to treat others the way I want to be treated.

The clear, negative, and unkind message of exasperation or pointing out mistakes is "You're an idiot and I'm really frustrated with you." Hopefully we don't say that out loud. We may not even realize that is what we're saying, even at arm's length—for example, pulling up fast behind the slowpoke car to make the point that he's slowing down traffic—but that *is* what we're saying.

Here are some of the many ways exasperation can be expressed. Recognize any?

- ☐ Correcting in an irritated fashion. ("Honey, the diaper tab does *not* fasten well that way.")
- ☐ Pointing out someone's mistake so she sees that she made one.
- ☐ Showing impatience by rolling our eyes, sighing, or grumbling.
- ☐ Getting frustrated easily or taking little mistakes personally ("This is the second time I've had to look at this, and it isn't even finished!") instead of calmly stating the facts ("It looks like that wasn't done correctly. Let's have you try that again. I know you'll do better next time.")
- ☐ Raising your voice in annoyance or anger.
- ☐ Saying or implying, "What were you thinking?"
- ☐ Saying someone's name in a frustrated way. ("Bonnie! You know we don't do it that way!")
- ☐ Saying, "You always . . ." or "You never . . ."
- ☐ Escalating when provoked. ("Well, if you're not going to do it right, don't come whining to me when you need help!")
- ☐ _____
- ☐ _____

In most cases, these reactions come from losing perspective. A good friend described an argument with her fifteen-year-old son. He is a really good, thoughtful kid, but he tends to lose things. In the last school year, he has misplaced a phone, a gym bag, and a pair of shoes—each of which required not only money (which he partially paid) but time she couldn't afford to drive around and replace everything. Then one day he again came home from the gym without his gym bag. She said, "I thought he was too cavalier about it, and

I exploded." After several minutes of arguing, he stomped away and she spent a few minutes steaming to a friend via text about what had just happened, about her son's irresponsibility, and so on.

Her friend wrote back, "I'm so sorry you're going to have to trail around to replace everything again. That must be so frustrating." There was a pause and then her friend sent another text. "But your son is not on drugs, he's healthy, and he loves Jesus."

My friend broke down in tears, and she and her son apologized to each other. She said, "I had totally lost perspective. When it comes down to it, I realize my anger and exasperation happen because I'm being inconvenienced. And yes, it is so frustrating and is a weakness of his. But he's a fifteen-year-old kid, and he's sensitive and tries hard to please. It's okay to express disappointment and give consequences. But when I explode like that I'm saying, 'My money, effort, and convenience are more important than your precious heart.'"

Ouch. So often, that is what I, too, am saying. And I'm not alone. In fact, *many* of those in the study did not originally see exasperation or irritation as particularly negative; to them it was just a sign of their own frustration, not a sign of unkindness toward another person. But once they had to start being purposely kind, it loomed large.

One woman did the 30-Day Kindness Challenge for her ten-year-old son. She adored him and had sacrificed a lot to homeschool him, but she admitted she also got impatient easily.

> When I started being attuned to this issue, I saw that there have been those times when he's spilled a glass of milk, and he's looked at me almost cowering, like, "Oh man, Mom's going to be so mad!" And it was like being punched in the stomach. I saw the effects of my anger leaking out on him when it never should have been. So I've been really working on not being negative or irritated. For example, after dinner, if he leaves his plate on the table instead of

taking it to the kitchen like he knows he should, I used to get
irritated and say, "Ben, you know you're supposed to take your plate.
Why did you leave that there?" and so on. But now I say, "Oh, Ben,
it looks like you forgot your plate," instead of dragging in all the
emotion of why did he or why didn't he. I just state the fact. And it
is really clear that some of the changes that have happened with me
are positively impacting him. He's just a happier child now. He's
much more open, affectionate, and willing to admit when he's done
something wrong.

☺

When we nix that negative, we are irritated less and enjoy the other person more.

I've discovered personally the truth that I've seen in my studies: if you don't
make a point of irritably stating what someone missed, it won't bother you as
much. If you don't make a point of pulling up behind the slower car, you'll be
more patient. And if you *do* make a point of speaking with kindness and patience, even when you're ready to scream, you'll want to scream a lot less.

When you work to eradicate exasperation and irritation in any environment—
home, school, the workplace, social media—we've found that these things
happen:

- You become less judgmental and more appreciative.
- You are more thoughtful and less reactive.
- You enjoy and/or accept someone for who they are, as they are.
- You enjoy life more and have greater peace and contentment.
- Those around you are happier.
- Those around you trust you more and are less guarded.
- Those around you are more likely to admit mistakes or wrongdoing.
- You add to peace in the world, instead of adding to the negative cycle
  of irritation.

3. Sarcasm

Our family is competitive, so we enjoy good-natured trash-talking when playing sports, games, or doing any other competitive endeavor. ("Oh yeah? Well you're so slow it takes you half an hour to make Minute Rice.") We know we love each other, so we can tease a bit and enjoy it. I also like snappy, sarcastic commentary just as much as the next person.

Until I don't. There comes a point at which it is actually tiring and no longer feels good natured or well intentioned.

And let's admit to ourselves that sometimes our sarcasm is not good natured at all, such as when we cut down another person either directly or by talking about them when they aren't around.

Do you find yourself using any of the following regularly?

- ☐ Sarcastic thoughts or comments.
- ☐ Witty rejoinders or amusing comebacks that put someone in their place.
- ☐ Semi-disparaging teasing.
- ☐ Very frequent good-natured teasing.
- ☐ Trash-talking.
- ☐ Cynicism (or, as one person put it, "the caricature of realism").
- ☐ Teasing, talking, or speaking sarcastically to or about someone in a way that makes them feel bad—or would if they heard it.
- ☐ _____
- ☐ _____

In an environment with total goodwill (where people know with 100 percent certainty that the other person cares about them), some teasing and trash-talking can be fun. Without total goodwill, it gets destructive fast. And even _with_ total goodwill, it gets tiring if it happens a lot.

Mandy already had an exhausting, challenging life and didn't realize her whole family's tendency toward funny, sarcastic comments was making it worse. With a special-needs teenage son who required a great deal of care and attention and a daughter starting college, she and her husband were just hanging on when she started the 30-Day Kindness Challenge. Here's how she put her revelation:

> We've always spoken in sarcasm. It is a way of protecting ourselves.
> Like, you either have to cry or laugh at some of what we go through,
> and I'd rather laugh! But when I started the 30-Day Kindness Chal-
> lenge, I found pretty quickly that being sarcastic was my way of
> being negative. Sarcasm doesn't have to be mean to be a problem.
> My husband's sarcasm is smart and funny, but after a while it is
> exhausting. It's also a barrier to depth.
>
> For example, if there's something to do with our son that would
> otherwise be an emotional topic—how we deal with his behavior or
> the pain of hospitalization—instead of addressing how we feel about
> it, we will joke or go to some very shallow place. And then we're unable
> to really share how we feel about him and raising him. We're always
> wearing masks.
>
> That was the main thing that changed when I started trying to
> avoid negative comments. I'm trying to speak sincerely instead, and it
> has changed my relationships. I'm more willing to let my husband or
> other people know how I'm really feeling instead of brushing them
> off. People would say, "You know, we're in awe of you guys, how you're
> dealing with all this stuff in raising your son," and we would always
> make light of it or make a sarcastic joke like, "Well, you didn't see us
> this morning!" So now we're trying to truly say, "Thanks. That means
> a lot to us." And it makes a huge difference in how we feel. There's a
> complete paradigm shift when you stop ignoring those compliments.
> We had to be willing to acknowledge we are *not* a normal family, and
> we're not perfect, but we're doing okay! We need to be able to celebrate
> the wins. It is so much better to focus on what we can be grateful for.

Mandy's family sarcasm showed primarily in quick and funny comments, and many similar people I've spoken to do not want to lose their sense of humor. But if they have a cutting wit, they realize the wit is fine but the cutting part may need to be used more sparingly and sensitively.

And of course, other types of sarcasm are not nearly so well intentioned to begin with; the more negative the tone, the meaner and more damaging it is— *especially* if it is done behind someone's back. As one teenager put it, "If a classmate is being all sarcastic about someone else to me, I have no doubt in my mind that she will rip me to someone else. So when I notice that a particular person never does that, I trust them a lot more."

When we nix that negative, we gain closeness with others and gratitude within ourselves.

Once sarcasm stops (or is used less frequently, only in well-intentioned ways, and never behind someone's back), people have consistently reported these results:

- People trust and like you more; they open up to you instead of keeping themselves closed off and at a distance.
- You are more likely to learn someone's honest judgment or opinion at home or at work.
- Among those with whom you have a personal, caring relationship, the walls come down; you are much more likely to vulnerably share real feelings and find that others share their feelings with you, developing true intimacy and closeness.
- You see much more of the positive: those things worth affirming, celebrating, and applauding.
- You experience greater gratitude.
- It changes the mood of your home, school, friendships, business, or other environments.

4. Grumble, Grumble

All of us feel dissatisfied sometimes. We focus on what should be rather than seeing the good we already have. We grumble over what isn't right and miss what is. We criticize the way something is being handled—or even beat ourselves up over how *we* handled it. But those attitudes quickly make us remarkably unkind, and it is usually in a way we are completely blind to. After all, very few of us think of ourselves as grumbling, grouchy, critical, dissatisfied, or discontented.

I certainly didn't. Most of those I've interviewed don't. Over the years I've always found it amusing to hear the answer when I ask someone, "Are you a glass-half-full or glass-half-empty sort of person?" Inevitably, those who are not glass-half-full types will pause and answer gravely, "I would say I'm more of a realist."

Well, guess what? It turns out that every single one of us has those "realistic" tendencies at times. Especially, I think, those with strong personalities. As one woman told me with a groan,

> I'm a Type A kind of person, and we have a lot of stress with that "Don't say anything negative" thing. It's because we have this tendency not even to *see* the positive as much as the negative. I don't lean toward noticing and saying, "Wow, you did great at that." Instead I tend to see and comment, "Here's what you didn't do." My previous husband used to protest that I was always focusing on what he did wrong. And I would just think, *Well, those are the facts. What's the problem?* Until I took this Challenge, I had no clue how much I criticize. I get on my boyfriend, my assistant, the guy who is working on my house . . . even myself!

Which of the following do you find yourself saying or doing?
- ☐ Thinking or saying, "I want it *this* way, not *that* way."
- ☐ Noticing problems, what wasn't done, what is not being done "right," or what isn't likely to work.

- ☐ Discounting the good that came before, because what is happening right now isn't quite up to snuff.
- ☐ Wondering, *What have you done for me lately?*
- ☐ Speaking in a dissatisfied tone (or speaking to your partner less kindly than you would a close friend).
- ☐ Thinking, *Things would be so much better if she just did this instead of this.*
- ☐ Thinking or saying, "What was he *thinking*?"
- ☐ Beating yourself up over what you did or didn't do.
- ☐ Emphasizing that the current situation is difficult. ("I'm exhausted." "The kids are so demanding." "Working with these people drives me nuts.")
- ☐ Saying, "I wish I didn't [feel sick, have to do more work than Jerry, have a husband who plays Xbox for hours, come home to see toys strewn all over the floor]."
- ☐ Saying, "I wish I did [have a wife who wanted sex more often, live in a better neighborhood, have a pet]."
- ☐ Saying, "But so-and-so won't [buy me that pet, advocate for me, care about my needs, talk to me]."
- ☐ _____
- ☐ _____

Don't get me wrong: there are reasons we might be well within our rights to feel concerned or irritated. Our hurts, worries, or preferences may be very legitimate. The problem is the pattern of response.

I loved a comment on my Facebook page in response to my asking, "How do you feel about the concept that you can't have it all, all at the same time?" One woman wisely pointed out, "This reminds me of when any of us says, 'I want to be happy.' How do you know that you are not already happy? It isn't about having everything. . . . It is about appreciating what you have and being thankful."

How do you know that you are not already happy? As we said earlier, it is a decision. And there's a reason the Bible talks about finding contentment no matter what is going on:[8] discontentment not only makes you unhappy yourself, but it also makes you unkind to others. You may feel negative, upset with yourself, and grumpy, but when you choose to act and speak positively, your feelings (and kindness) will follow.

My husband, Jeff, is my hero in this way. He admits he has that glass-half-empty tendency in his personality, and frankly there's much that could drive him nuts about living with me. He's a very neat person and I seem to be missing that gene. It makes perfect sense to me for clothes to be piled on top of the dresser instead of in the drawers. Yet somewhere along the way I noticed that he stopped getting frustrated about that or about how quickly the kids and I can turn his neat living room into an explosion of Legos, schoolbooks, scattered shoes, and electronic devices. When I asked what changed, he said, "I started to look at all that stuff and think, *That is a sign that I have a wife and two amazing kids living in this house.* So it becomes a gift."

When we nix that negative, we gain more enjoyment of what we have.
I was glad to see that among those who did the 30-Day Kindness Challenge, habits of discontentment dropped dramatically—and dissatisfaction dropped along with it! For example, among women who did the Challenge for their husband or boyfriend, the majority started by admitting that they spoke less kindly to their men than they did to their close friends. After the Challenge, the pattern was exactly the opposite, with 82 percent saying their tone with their partner was the same as or even better than with their close friends.

When you learn the secret of contentment and force yourself to stop dissatisfied thoughts, words, and actions, you'll see these results:

- You see and appreciate the good things and people in your life so much more. You enjoy, celebrate, and value what you *do* have.
- You enjoy the moment instead of missing it. ("The kids are only small once." "I'm going to learn everything I can at this job while I'm here.")

- You live in a sense of awe. (Instead of, *I have to do this job,* you think, *I get to do this job.*)
- You're more optimistic overall (contentment leads to enjoyment, which leads to optimism).
- You're in a good mood more often.

5. You Hurt Me, I Hurt You

Few people think of themselves as bitter. But look at how the Oxford dictionary defines the word: "Angry, hurt, or resentful [of people or their feelings or behavior] because of one's bad experiences or a sense of unjust treatment."[9] Suddenly, we may need to ask ourselves whether we are, in fact, dealing with bitterness in a relationship.

Remember the story of Sarah and her live-in mother? The existence of bitterness isn't only signaled by a lifelong vendetta. If you feel a sense of anger, hurt, or resentment toward someone because of something they have done, that type of negativity can impact your ability to be positive and kind. Without your purposeful effort to combat those feelings, they will likely bubble over in irritation, tension, and outright anger or come out in back-room venting or discussion with others.

Do any of these seem familiar in your life? (Check off or write these down as well as others that occur to you.)

☐ Repeatedly being annoyed or irritated by someone at home, at the office, or elsewhere.

☐ Repeatedly being angry or upset about what someone said or did.

☐ Pondering or replaying past hurts or negative incidents in your mind or out loud. ("They did this, and then this is what happened next.")

☐ Venting to someone else about a specific person or group. ("Just getting it off my chest.")

- ☐ Impulsively expressing (via e-mail, text, phone call, or online post) irritation, anger, or hurt.
- ☐ Complaining to someone about their words or behavior.
- ☐ Having difficulty forgiving.
- ☐ Pulling away, shutting down, or checking out of a conversation, activity, or other part of someone's life.
- ☐ Cutting off contact, declining to return e-mails or calls, or uninviting someone from social media.
- ☐ _____
- ☐ _____

Among those who did the 30-Day Kindness Challenge for a partner, *two-thirds* said their tendency to talk about their partner's faults declined.

They Nixed the Negative

The survey measured participants' agreement with this statement: "I sometimes talk about my partner's faults with others." From before to after the 30-Day Kindness Challenge, participants:

Improved (They talked less with others about their partner's faults.)	66%
No change (They talked the same amount about their partner's faults.)	25%
Worsened (They talked more about their partner's faults.)	10%

Something else happened too: participants started to see their own issues. One international participant had done the 30-Day Kindness Challenge for his mother, who had divorced his father when he was young. As an adult he found himself frequently irritated with and complaining about his mom and her frequent excuses that she was "too tired" to come to his town to help with his children, even though she sincerely wanted a good relationship with the family.

During the Challenge, he realized that much of his irritation stemmed from both unforgiveness and a one-sided focus:

> Through this process I've become more conscious of my own faults, not just those of my mum. It is quite easy for kids to see the faults of their parents. But it is more difficult to see your own faults in how you have treated your parents. This has reminded me she did a lot for us growing up, taking care of us on her own. There's a lot to be thankful for. If I'm honest, I've let her down. It will make a difference to tell her that and ask for forgiveness. But it also makes a difference for me, since the realization that I had messed up hasn't even been a category of thought for me until now.

When we nix that negative, we get greater peace and more purpose.
We've seen that when you confront the negativity arising from anger or hurt, these things tend to happen:

- You have more peace of mind because you avoid the torture of reliving it.
- You end up with compassion and understanding instead of anger.
- You appreciate others for the past, current, or potential positives they offer.
- You move toward constructive solutions.
- You see your own faults, not just theirs.
- You forgive.

6. Suspicion

Suspicion is sneaky because by definition it often seems justified. And sometimes it is. If your study partner repeatedly assures you that she is almost done with her part of the big project, yet her roommate casually mentions that she's been out partying for days, you would be justified in suspecting her progress. If your husband repeatedly assures you that you're the only one for him and yet you find a note from a stranger saying, "Can't wait to see you again," then, yes, it is completely legitimate to be suspicious!

But in most cases it isn't. When we're suspicious, we usually believe the worst of people's intentions, even when they care for us very much. We view people's words and actions in the worst light rather than looking for a more generous (and usually more accurate) explanation. Suspicion worms its way inside our hearts and comes out of our mouths as negativity.

Do you recognize any of these words or thoughts?

- ☐ "My coworker said he just forgot to copy me about the meeting, but I don't think he wanted me there."
- ☐ "The boss is keeping me out of the loop, isn't he?"
- ☐ "She complimented me only because she had to, not because she meant it."
- ☐ "No, she wasn't trying to help! She was trying to make me feel bad."
- ☐ "She couldn't care less about me. That's why she said/did/didn't do that."
- ☐ "I couldn't reach you. Where were you? Who did you have lunch with? When did they invite you?"
- ☐ "Were you just checking out that woman?"
- ☐ "I think he works so many hours only because he enjoys work more than being with our family."
- ☐ "He knew how that would make me feel and he said it anyway."
- ☐ "She knew if she could just keep us distracted we wouldn't hear the coach and she would win. That's the only reason she was being so friendly."
- ☐ "He said he wants to change, but he's not going to."
- ☐ _____
- ☐ _____

This list can go on forever since a suspicious, negative mind-set tends to feed on itself. And as noted in chapter 4, what you watch for, you will find. If you think your coworker didn't want you at that meeting, then (in your mind) that means he doesn't like or appreciate you as a colleague, so you now watch for other signals that confirm that. His most innocent comments ("Let's hustle through this because I know we all want to get home at a good hour tonight") are perceived through the worst possible lens ("He hates working on this project with us"). You start snapping at him or going around him since you don't trust him. Then he gets irritated and perhaps responds in kind, which only reinforces your now full-blown suspicions. And so on.

Believing the worst of people kills collegial work relationships, friendships, and marriages that never had to die.

When we nix that negative, we will see the positive, encouraging truth that was there all along.

The quickest way to counteract this deadly form of negativity is to ask God to open your eyes to the truth and then look for a more generous explanation of words or behavior that concern you. In most cases you'll find it, which will encourage you, which will make it so much easier to nix the negative thoughts next time.

For example, you might realize that your husband doesn't really like work more than family time but simply feels burdened by the large student loan debt you two have to pay off. Perhaps you see that your friend felt she had to raise that difficult issue (however imperfectly) in order to preserve your friendship rather than trash it. In other words, she said that particular thing because she *does* care about you. It won't always work that way, of course, but seeing those truths when they are there will help you keep that positive perspective for the next time.

7. Catastrophizing

In doing this research I discovered that I am a champ at a type of negativity I didn't previously know existed: catastrophizing.

Does anything on this list describe a pattern of word or thought?

- [ ] "If such and such happens, it will be a catastrophe."
- [ ] "The team is making a baaaaad decision, and I can see the train wreck coming!"
- [ ] Expecting doom in issues such as the economy, personal finances, racial dynamics, office intrigue, injustice, a group or culture going the "wrong" direction, or anything else that sparks the feeling that things are falling apart—or might if we don't do something about it.
- [ ] Assuming the proposal, idea, or suggestion will never work.
- [ ] "If you don't get better grades, you are never getting into a good college."
- [ ] "That person or group is going to ruin [our business, the country, my kids' grades, the campus, her family, the economy]."
- [ ] "If so-and-so is/isn't elected, life as we know it is over."
- [ ] "If we don't act on [global warming, education, religious liberties], irreversible damage will be done."
- [ ] "It will be a disaster if he [doesn't stop playing so many video games, takes that job, marries that girl]."
- [ ] After pondering mistreatment, a grievance, or injustice, saying, "This isn't right!" or "How dare they?"
- [ ] Being attuned to what is fair or unfair.
- [ ] Pondering how to get revenge or make things right.
- [ ] Getting in arguments about any of these issues (what the Bible calls "being quarrelsome").
- [ ] _____
- [ ] _____

Many of us might look at this list and think, *But it* would *indeed be a disaster if some of those things happened!* I'm not disputing that. The problem is that trying to prevent (or solve) the disaster tends to make us remarkably unkind—without, in some cases, even realizing it. And let's also admit that in some cases our minds build up a potential catastrophe that never unfolds. Even if it did, our reaction sometimes creates a worse problem for us than the one we are worried about.

One woman I spoke to completed the 30-Day Kindness Challenge for her husband, trying to save her fairly new second marriage from falling apart under the weight of challenges related to his health issues, her young daughters, and lots of business travel. She said,

> I've always struggled with control and being *the* parent in charge of the girls. And now I have a partner who is more than willing and capable of contributing, and I have to back off. That is scary because I automatically think, *But what if he doesn't get it right? I have these two little souls here!* I would jump in and essentially push him aside, which basically tells him, "You don't know what you're doing. You're an idiot." It would hurt this great guy. This Challenge made me realize I'm unkind because I don't trust. When I don't trust my husband's way, this evil whisper in my heart says, *He's doing it again and it will be bad.* But when I force myself to shut that down and look for the positive, we are much more likely to talk about it, come to agreement, and affirm that we're still walking this path together. I think God blesses that.

This type of negativity also risks acts of unkindness that may or may not impact our own personal lives but certainly will impact the lives of the people we're reacting to. When we are aggrieved, it is all too easy to become what some have labeled a "crybully." If we feel that we are protecting or fighting against something dangerous, we are passionate and on edge. It becomes a personal mission to help make sure the existing or approaching catastrophe is solved or avoided, and in the heat of the moment other considerations—politeness, self-restraint, unconditional love, care for others' feelings, respect—are too easily swept away.

And let's be very honest. In the heat of the moment, sometimes it feels good to let all that anger or indignation out. Somewhere deep down we know our methods are unkind, even cruel, but we ignore that knowledge because of course we feel so justified! And embracing that justification feels so good too. A *Wall Street Journal* article put it well: As we become crybullies, "the pleasures of aggression [are] added to the comforts of feeling aggrieved."[10]

Yet we can have high standards and expectations without being harsh. We can press for crucial solutions in our marriages and be kind at the same time. We can fight the good fight against dangerous trends or for causes we care about while still being respectful of those with whom we disagree. *They* may not be respectful, but we can be.

And doing so prevents us from becoming people we do not want to be. I am quite sure that hours, days, or even years later, at least some percentage of the population privately considers things they have said—texts sent in anger, impulsive online posts, furious comments made to a political adversary—and been ashamed of themselves. Even though I try to be a kind person, there are times when I look back and wonder how I could have ever said or done something so unkind. There are times when I wonder how I could have spent so much time getting into what the Bible bluntly calls "foolish and stupid arguments."[11]

:)

When we nix that negative, we'll experience more enjoyment and a lighter heart as well as free ourselves to find constructive solutions.

You'll be surprised at the mental and emotional shift that occurs when you force yourself, for thirty days, *not* to get into foolish arguments or focus on or talk about a potential catastrophe. Here are some of the many positive outcomes I have heard:

- You are much more relaxed and at peace, instead of worrying that the world will fall apart or feeling that everything is on your shoulders.

- You experience more enjoyment and more fun since you're not focused on how things are dreadful, awful, or falling apart.
- You discover a heart change; you are more positive and lighthearted in general.
- You practice greater trust in God.
- You give God a chance to change someone's heart rather than feeling it is up to you.[12]
- You discover constructive, creative solutions.
- You become a true leader rather than a bomb thrower or an unhelpful contrarian.

None of this means that we can't address something that might be a potential problem that matters to us, our business, our school, our family, or the culture. But it does mean that we need to address it in a purposefully positive, constructive, and kind way.

King David did this. In the Old Testament book of 1 Samuel, we see that despite the fact that David was the rightful king of Israel and had served the current king (Saul) with true devotion, Saul and his troops hunted David in the wilderness. A motley gang of disaffected, alienated men joined David—men who had been unfairly driven from regular society. These men had every right to be aggrieved and to demand justice and change. They were truly aching for "the pleasures of aggression" against Saul.

But David wouldn't do it. He commanded that no one touch the Lord's anointed king. He modeled kindness. He demonstrated trust that God would care for them. And what happened? Instead of forcing change, those disaffected men themselves were changed. They became David's "mighty men."[13] And when God eventually made the way for David to become king, those mighty men became the most powerful force for true righteousness and justice in the kingdom.

HAVING EYES FILLED WITH LIGHT

Jesus repeatedly emphasized something vital to our resolve against negativity: this world *is* negative and dark, but he is the "light of the world" and our job is to shine that light to transform the darkness.[14] Where there is discontentment, we are to bring peace. Where we want to be impatient, we must be patient instead. Where the world is harsh, we are to be gentle.

How do we do this? We need Jesus's light and love ourselves in order to share it with others. We cannot give what we do not have. But then, he said, we must also have something else: a focus on the light amid the darkness:

> No one lights a lamp and puts it in a place where it will be hidden, or under a bowl. Instead they put it on its stand, so that those who come in may see the light. Your eye is the lamp of your body. When your eyes are healthy, your whole body also is full of light. But when they are unhealthy, your body also is full of darkness. See to it, then, that the light within you is not darkness. Therefore, if your whole body is full of light, and no part of it dark, it will be just as full of light as when a lamp shines its light on you.[15]

In other words, what we notice, see, and focus on (our eye) is what will either illuminate our whole being or darken it. If what we see and say is full of light and positivity, *we* will be full of light and positivity. But if what we notice, see, and say is dark, dissatisfied, critical, sarcastic, irritated, suspicious, or angry, we ourselves will be all those things. We are charged to focus on the light, not the dark.

What you look for you will find. We'll be seeing a lot more of that (no pun intended!) as we unpack Element #2 in the next chapter.

Practice Praise

Overcoming Ten Tricky Traps

> *Element #2* Every day, find one positive thing that you can sincerely praise or affirm about your person and tell them, and tell someone else.

Some time ago, Jeff and I interviewed a pastor and his wife while we were in New England conducting a weekend seminar series on marriage, youth, and parenting. This couple was effective at restoring broken marriages, so Jeff and I asked their secret. I had not yet told this couple—whom I will call Samuel and Sierra—about my kindness research, so I was intrigued by their immediate answer: "Whenever we hear one person say something good about the other, we pass it along."

Samuel explained,

Years ago I heard a story about how a young man solved a conflict between two church elders who had been friends but now couldn't stand each other. One day, one of them said something negative about the other one behind his back, and the young man said, "He is a really good businessman, though," and the guy grudgingly agreed. So the young guy went to the other elder and said, "You know, Tom said you're a good businessman." He was taken aback. "Really?" The young guy made some small talk, then said, "And you have to admit, Tom's a really good dad." Then he told Tom, "He said you're a good dad." He went back and forth a few times and pretty soon the guys started bringing the walls down and found their friendship again. I realized encouraging words help anyone, but they're especially important with people who are in a difficult place in marriage.

Sierra added,

If Samuel and I are working with a negative couple, we try to bring up anything positive. For example, Keshia was a wife who corrected people a lot, and her husband, Ben, was a negative person. In the lobby one day he was complaining about how she was always late, and I said, "She does a lot for you, though, doesn't she?" and he said, "I could not live without her." He gave some details. I then went to Keshia and told her Ben had praised those things—and she didn't believe me! She had never heard those nice things from him.

Then I complimented her on this cool leather bag she had. She explained Ben's an artisan and makes some things specially for her. I said, "He does a good job on that, doesn't he?" and she said he does. When I shared that with him, he was stunned she said anything good about him. Then I started bringing out other things over the next week or two, like character traits. And once he heard that his wife had said, "He's a man of great integrity," he broke down in Samuel's office. He had no idea she felt anything but disdain for him.

We challenged her to keep simply appreciating him without correcting him. And we challenged him to find those things to praise and *tell* her. People just aren't encouraging others with their words. So I listen, and I share their words to get them started. Of course, sometimes I have to be direct. I will put them on the love seat in my office and say, "You have to come up with ten compliments to tell each other before you can leave the room." And they will say dumb things at first like, "She has blond hair," "He has blue eyes." But by the end they are saying genuine things. It may take some practice, but over time they will find them.

Samuel added,

It becomes a good habit. One woman we worked with said she later told a clerk at Walmart, "You work so quickly; you're amazing." And he said, "No one has ever said that to me before." She was so pleased. Once you start down this road, you'll want to keep going. It is very satisfying.

Praise Is the Catalyst of Kindness

The practice of praise *is* very satisfying. It is also the catalyst of kindness.

Have you ever used those little hand warmers when the weather is freezing? Open up the vacuum-sealed packaging, expose the small pouch to air, and . . . *aaaaahhh.* Oxygen chemically reacts with the iron powder inside the pouch to produce instant soothing warmth on a cold day. A simple reaction creates a welcome result.

Our praise of others is like the oxygen. It is the active element that sparks a chemical reaction, radiating warmth and kindness toward a cold heart, relationship, or culture. All types of negativity act a bit like the plastic packaging— like a barrier around the heart that prevents the reaction from occurring. This is one reason eliminating negativity is so crucial. But once affirmation, praise, and appreciation flood in, the reaction begins. Positivity and praise mix with small acts of generosity to create kindness. The sort of kindness that is transformational for each of us and for everyone around us.

In other words, if kindness has power, sincere affirmation is the power behind the power.

If you want proof that praise is a key catalyst in changing things for the better—for the other person, for the relationship, *and* for you—look no further than what happened to the group in our study that started off at the worst end of the praise scale and ended up at the best.

Among those who did the 30-Day Kindness Challenge for a romantic partner, there was a small group of two dozen men and women who disclosed on the survey that they rarely or never praised their partner in the week before the Challenge started, but by the time the Challenge ended they were giving daily praise.

Not surprisingly, all their metrics improved. For example, they were happier in their relationships and felt they were far more likely to last a lifetime. But the most gratifying result was this: *they themselves felt much more loved and appreciated by their partners.*

In most of those cases, with only a few exceptions, their partner was not involved or even aware of the Challenge! The person doing the Challenge was doing all the work. And yet by the end of one short month, three of four felt far more loved and appreciated—an exact reversal from where they started!

And this trend was clear even beyond those most in need of it. Among those with *any* room for improvement, fully two-thirds felt more loved and appreciated after doing the full Challenge! Perhaps even more dramatic, you may remember from chapter 3 that among those in the overall group who did the Challenge, 74 percent said their partners changed for the better. Not that they themselves had changed (although they had), but that *the other person* had changed. And among the group who moved from little or no praise to daily praise, the number rose to 92 percent! Remember, most of their partners *did not take the Challenge.* But the person who did saw them change anyway, and they themselves felt more loved and appreciated in the end. Clearly, praise needs to be a priority.

Show More Care, Feel More Cared For

Among those who went from giving little or no praise to giving daily praise.

How much do you generally feel loved and appreciated by your partner?
"I feel..."

	Before Challenge	After Challenge
Very loved and appreciated	12.5%	50%
Quite loved and appreciated	12.5%	29%
Do feel loved and appreciated	**25%**	**79%**
Middle of the road—sometimes I feel loved and appreciated, sometimes I don't	50%	21%
Not particularly loved and appreciated	17%	0%
Not at all loved and appreciated	8%	0%
Don't feel loved and appreciated	**75%**	**21%**
Total	**100%**	**100%**

Note: Among those who went from expressing appreciation "Never" or "Once or twice a week" the week before the 30-Day Kindness Challenge to expressing appreciation "Daily or more" after thirty days.

OVERCOMING TRAPS, DISHING OUT PRAISE, AND THE BENEFITS OF DOING SO

Everyone agrees in theory that affirmation is a good thing. Yet when challenged to practice it on a daily basis, we encounter all sorts of obstacles and objections. Much as we may not have realized that exasperation is a form of negativity we need to eradicate (see the last chapter!), we may not have realized that we aren't giving the type of praise needed by those in our lives. Yet we must give it if we are to improve our relationship and be a part of a cultural movement of kindness.

Praise goes far beyond "Good job" and encompasses *whatever makes the people in your life feel affirmed*. It has to be sincere and genuine on your part, of course, but what matters is what they see as meaningful praise, whether or not you see it that way. This is not an exhaustive list, but true praise includes spoken or written phrases like:

- "Good job this week."
- "Thank you for doing that."
- "I'm grateful for your [willingness, candor, thoughtfulness, courage]."
- "Your investment of [time, a skill, resources, prayer, humor] will make a huge difference."
- "He told me what you did. I really appreciate that."
- "They loved your presentation."
- "You are so [efficient, productive, fast, good] at this."
- "Well done."
- "This team would not be the same without you."
- "You're a good man."
- "You're a wonderful mom."
- "I love your heart to help others, honey."
- "You make me so happy."
- "You are so beautiful, sweetheart."
- "I love your outfit. You've got great fashion sense!"
- "You're a great friend."
- "I really like spending time with you."
- "You're a really special person."
- "Jack and Tricia told me how much they [respect, like, appreciate] you."

To be a person of praise, you'll need to keep these kinds of affirmations on your tongue and in your e-mails, notes, text messages, and posts to or about others every day, multiple times a day.

If you're anything like me, you've realized that you want to do more of this than you actually do. Quite a few common factors get in the way, hold us back, or make us less than praise happy. So let's dig up some courage and identify what we may need to overcome, what we should be doing, and what happens when we do. As before, read with a pen in hand and check or make

Question to Consider
How am I doing at saying those phrases regularly to the people I most care about? How about to the people with whom I need a better relationship?

notes on any obstacles or factors that apply to you and which you most want or need to work on.

1. Say "Thank You" Even If It's for Something the Person Is "Supposed" to Do

One of the most important ways to practice praise is to get in the habit of saying, "Thank you." Everyone loves to hear those words, and statistically they are especially life giving for men. (In my book *For Women Only,* you can see more about how "thank you" is a man's equivalent of "I love you.")

Yet when I have shared the importance of thanks, I've often seen puzzlement or even indignation. As one mom asked, "Why should I thank my son for unloading the dishwasher when he is just doing his job?" One senior manager shrugged and told me, "Yes, I say thanks if I think about it. But their compensation is their thanks, right?" Another woman, challenged to thank her husband more regularly, was much more irritated. "Oh yippee," she said, rolling her eyes. "Get out the balloons for the praise party!" When I probed to find out the reason for her intense (although not unusual) reaction, she indicated, "It is childish and unnecessary. He's a grownup."

Even those who enjoy giving praise may have this same subconscious thought. For example, you may have wondered, as you read the story I told in

Chapter 4, why I was disappointed that only one person thought to cheer the father carrying his four-year-old daughter down the Cliff Hanger slide. You may have thought, *But why should you have thought to cheer for him? He was only doing what any parent should do.*

All these responses misunderstand the nature of praise and the emotional necessity of being appreciated. A word of thanks or appreciation (or love or gratitude) may not be necessary in the same sense that water and food are necessary. But it is fuel all the same. It keeps you going emotionally in the same way that a paycheck does financially and food does physically. And it does the same for every single person around you, whether a given action is their responsibility or not. Because our culture is made up of people, these positive words keep our society going: they are essential if we want to transform the world in which we live.

I think most of us know the importance of praise and affirmation. After all, *we* want to be affirmed too. So we need to be honest with ourselves about one reason we sometimes fail to give affirmation: we feel entitled to whatever the other person is doing.

Jeff and I were talking about this recently, and he made a great point:

> I think we sometimes feel, *You owe this to me. I deserve what you're doing.* This means that one reason we don't praise is pride. Our focus is solely on ourselves. We don't recognize what is in others or what it costs them to do that action that benefits us—even if it *is* a duty. It is easy to forget that we really don't *deserve* anything. Everything God allows us to have is a gift, right? So it is all praiseworthy.

For any person in our lives—man or woman, spouse, child, teacher, supervisor, or employee—it can be easy to think, *I shouldn't have to say these words of affirmation.* But this is why we're doing the Kindness Challenge. Maybe you don't *have* to say anything, but it makes a big difference if you do.

It keeps others going. But here's what you might otherwise miss: it also keeps *you* going because you start to see even more good things than what you praised them for. In many cases, you start to see ways they give of themselves for you or others, actions you might have taken for granted or never even noticed before.

One woman, Carly, described how her frustration and annoyance with her live-in sister changed to mindfulness in a way she didn't expect:

> My older sister lives with us because we need a nanny and she needs a
> home. But there's been a personality conflict between us for the last
> ten years, so it is kind of sticky. When she does something around the
> house like cooking dinner, washing dishes, or baby-sitting the kids, I
> haven't treated them as actions that require a thank-you because they're
> part of her job—part of the agreement we have for her living with us.
> But I realized: you know, as a mom of preschoolers, I feel like I go
> unnoticed a lot. I'm sure she feels the same when I don't acknowledge
> what she does to help us.
>
> She also has arthritis and some other health issues. And since I've
> started being mindful to say thank you, I started to notice things, like
> the fact that she may be feeling bad, but when it is time for her to make
> dinner, she does it anyway. I know she makes a lot of sacrifices for us. I
> didn't really notice that before.

☺ **When we overcome this obstacle and practice praise, it so thoroughly changes the dynamic that we often receive the type of affirmation *we* need.**
When I asked Carly, "Did you see any differences in your sister or in your relationship?" she answered, "Without a doubt. We're more affectionate now. Growing up, we were always very loving. We would hug each other, would sit

together on the couch and pass a tub of ice cream back and forth while we were watching TV. But I've been thinking I just didn't do that anymore with my sister, and it was because of my bitterness toward her. And over these last few weeks I have noticed that affection coming back. That is something very welcome, honestly. I'm sure she has missed that too."

2. Give Respect Even If They Don't Deserve It

If you've been seriously hurt by someone, or if a particular person makes you absolutely furious, the idea of going beyond non-negativity and actually giving them praise might seem ludicrous. Perhaps you've been devastated by a spouse's betrayal or a boss's cruelty. Perhaps someone is so mean or incompetent that you spend a lot of time and energy opposing them. Or perhaps the person is simply distant or difficult and you remove yourself as much as possible. In any of those cases, it can be easy to wonder how—or whether—to suddenly turn around and praise this person.

There are certainly going to be cases where finding something worthy of praise is extraordinarily difficult. Delivering that praise may be even harder. The question is this: Do we want a better relationship with that other person and more peace in ourselves, and do we want to try to follow the way of Jesus? If the answer to any part of that question is yes, then we have to decide whether we are willing, as described in chapter 1, to treat them as we wish they were treating us. And if so, that means to not only eliminate negativity but to practice affirmation, as hard as that may be.

As I was beginning the research for this book, one of my friends was having an extremely difficult time with the coach of her thirteen-year-old son's travel soccer team. Her son is a skilled goalie with unusual potential, and the coach had promised, in order to recruit him, never to practice or play on Sundays. But the coach was soon scheduling Sunday games and cruelly telling her son that if he missed them his teammates would lose and it would be his fault. The coach also tended to use harsh, abusive language with the kids.

Furious, my friend confronted him. When he refused to change, she got more upset and harsh herself. Eventually, she realized she was being just as unkind to him as he was to the kids, the cycle was getting worse, and her son was watching and absorbing all of it as the norm for how one handles things.

Instead of pulling her son off the team—which would have caused other problems, since he was being evaluated and recruited for high-school teams—she changed how she related to this coach she thought of as despicable. She realized that she would have to not only eliminate the harsh rhetoric but also figure out how to treat this coach with some semblance of respect. She eventually discovered that the only way to do that was to always speak in a respectful tone and thank him for what he *did* do well for the kids, even as she continued to push him on what he didn't.

Remember: this does not mean to turn a blind eye to abusive patterns, to put up with terrible treatment, or to excuse incompetence. This mom continued to vigorously press this coach and the league to a higher standard until the day the season ended; she just refused to stoop to a lower standard herself while she did so. Her actions certainly changed her, even though she said that in the end they didn't change much about the coach! But she could tell that her son saw a very clear distinction between two different choices of how people could relate in the world—and which one he wanted to make his own.

Perhaps your situation is a workplace one; you might have determined that an employee is not suited for her role and you need to let her go. But when you have that difficult conversation, you use a respectful, kind tone. And you practice praise by finding things you appreciate so she knows where you think she would fit better in the future.

One business owner I know has a reputation for that sort of respect and kindness toward others even in a difficult situation. He runs a tight ship and has had to fire his fair share of those who couldn't cut it. And yet several of those terminated employees have given his name *as a reference* to their potential new employers! This business owner was so good at thinking through and offering affirmation for where these employees *were* strong that they wanted their future employers to talk to this man who had fired them. I thought that was extraordinary—and a mark of the type of leader we all should aspire to be.

But what about when there has been a more intense problem, such as a deep personal betrayal? Multiple people took the 30-Day Kindness Challenge to help heal a marriage suffering the effects of an affair. Some of those decided not to finish. But those who did usually saw a change that made the road to healing much easier. As one woman put it,

> My husband had an affair, so the last year has been rough. This Challenge helped me to move forward in a positive way. I never realized how often I've been saying negative things about him to others or how negatively I would approach things with him. It helped me see how much my attitude was affecting the reconciliation of our marriage and how many little affirmations were missing. Now that I have been more positive, I see him doing little things like telling me he loves me first, waiting for me instead of walking ahead of me, sending me texts during the day, and talking to me about his day in the evening. I am so grateful.

☺ **When we overcome this obstacle and practice praise, not only does the relationship usually get better; it helps set *us* free.**
If we are thinking, *My boss/spouse/friend doesn't deserve my praise,* that's a signal we have been deeply wounded by them in some way. And most of us know that if we've been wounded, the key to being free is forgiveness. That can be a hard thing to do, but praise can help us get there.

3. Build a Bridge When You'd Rather Battle

Let's just admit that sometimes people get under our skin. Or maybe just one particular person does. Maybe we're tired, stressed, or angry in a way that has nothing to do with them. Or maybe it has everything to do with them! Regardless, when we're angry, sometimes it just feels better to do battle than build a bridge. In the moment, at least.

And yet it is in that exact moment that kindness matters most. That is when we act like the kind person we have decided to be. Even if everything in us wants to say "Bring it on" instead!

I interviewed Mya one week after she completed the 30-Day Kindness Challenge to heal a difficult relationship with her mother-in-law, whom she and her husband relied on for daily childcare for their twin daughters but who had a hurtful tendency to use passive-aggressive behavior. When I said to Mya, "So you finished the Challenge a week ago. How has the last week been?" I was amused by her answer:

Ah. Um. Funny you asked. Literally the day after the Challenge ended, she did something that pushed all my buttons. The girls were home with my husband since he didn't have to work that day. His mom called me at work but I was in a meeting. Later I got a voice mail that said, "Well, I wanted to invite you to lunch, but you were much too busy to answer my phone call. So I went to this fabulous place and it was marvelous and I had a great time without you. I'm so sorry you were too busy to answer your phone." And the immature part of me thought, *Well, I'm really glad the Challenge is over* now!

I shouldn't have gotten my feelings hurt, but I did. But I'd learned during the thirty days that faking it until you feel it can be a great thing. You choose to behave positively and hopefully your feelings will follow your actions. So I left her a kind voice mail saying, "I'm so sorry I missed your call. I am glad you had fun!"

Responding that way gave me overnight to file my pride, put away my bitterness, and choose to be kind and not frosty. I don't want to be passive aggressive with her. Well . . . I *want* to, but I am going to choose *not* to. It's all about those actions. You can't always choose your feelings, but you can choose your behavior.

☺

When we overcome this obstacle and practice praise, we reduce conflict, experience more peace, and find that (eventually) our feelings will follow our actions.

There is an automatic benefit of less conflict when we exercise self-control and refuse to fight. And it isn't a false peace; it is real. As Mya explained, "I had actually found during the thirty days just how much it defuses a tense situation when you do something kind instead of insisting on having the last word. It is amazing what appreciation does to calm conflict and bring real reconciliation."

4. Notice the Good Things You Were Blind to Before

Maybe we're not itching for battle, we're just blind. The comment "I didn't really notice that before" is one of the most common phrases I hear in speaking with people who are doing the 30-Day Kindness Challenge. And it points out a main reason why the Challenge is so effective: not because it is any magic formula, but because it erases kindness blindness. It wakes us up to the good that was there all along but that we weren't giving someone credit for. Because if we weren't seeing it, we certainly weren't saying it!

At one telecom company, a woman named Renee described a common dynamic: "In my last job they simply didn't prioritize praise. Literally the only time a supervisor came by your station was when there was a problem and they were asking why calls took too long to resolve. They never looked for the instances when a client was so happy that they wrote in a great comment. It was as if our company was completely blind to the good unless you pointed it out. And after a while everyone gets tired of standing on a desk and shouting 'Look at me!' so the turnover was high."

She paused, then gave a rueful smile. "I love where I am now, but that experience made me so aware of things worth praising. When I'm on a customer site now, I'm almost *acutely* aware of making sure to say something positive at all times, because their environment is probably lacking that. Once we have awareness we have to act on it."

☺ **When we overcome this obstacle and practice praise in our difficult relationships, we start to see the praiseworthy everywhere.**
Even better, when we see and call out things we appreciate, we'll see more of it. Not to mention that others will sure appreciate us!

After Renee described her efforts to say positive things, her colleague nodded. "My old company was great at that. The president would stand on stage in the monthly leadership meetings and call out this guy or this gal in the meeting for something they had done great, and these people would have no idea that it had even been noticed. But once you know that others *see* the good things that are happening, it motivates them to do even better. When I see my director praise other people in the meeting on small things, it doesn't just show me he values affirmation; it also shows me he pays attention to what is happening in the business."

☐ 5. Tell Them You're Grateful Rather Than Assume They Know It

We often think that this other person, or group of people, already knows how we feel about them. And if they don't, they should.

Right?

This is a big one, and it probably affects every human being. I'm highly guilty of this with my staff and other close colleagues. I have a tremendous group of talented employees, contractors, and publishing partners who bust their tails for me. I *feel* tremendous gratitude for all of them. But can they feel what I feel? No. Does my longtime staff director, Linda, know that I just told someone I couldn't have accomplished half of what I've done without her? Does my amazing assistant, Theresa, know the gratitude I feel whenever a client picks me up at the airport and tells me how helpful she was? Can Caroline, my digital content manager, hear my thoughts of awe about how on earth she can stay on top of every smidge of social media content and still juggle parenting two kids in diapers?

There is no way someone else can actually know your appreciation, love, gratitude, or any other thought or feeling unless you tell him or her. (Does it make up for years of not saying it enough if you publish it in a book?)

Our studies over the years have shown that this is a particularly important issue for husbands to be aware of. Guys, the data shows that in most cases you adore your wives . . . but you also assume they know that. Think again. Not only can your wife not hear your thoughts; she probably has a subconscious question about whether she is truly lovable and loved. Our research showed that eight out of ten women on our nationally representative survey had an inner doubt that made them wonder, *Is he glad he married me? Would he choose me all over again?*

Men, you may think the hard work you do to provide for your wife and family is the most tangible expression of how much you care about her. You may be surprised to discover that statistically, the action that most tangibly says "I care about you" is your presence. And although your work to provide is appreciated, it also takes you *away* from her for many hours a day, so she is even more likely to need to actually hear your words of affection, appreciation, and gratitude. (If you're a husband who wants to do this Challenge for your wife, see chapter 9.)

☺ **When we overcome this obstacle and practice praise, we provide security for the other person, which benefits us as that person acts out of confidence rather than insecurity or hair-trigger sensitivity.**

For example, as your spouse sees your gratitude tangibly every day, he or she relaxes in *knowing* you care. You'll be amazed to look back and realize, *We haven't had much conflict lately.* Why? Well, for example, when your wife is certain you care, she no longer acts from insecurity. She no longer adds to conflict as she seeks resolution. She is able to reassure herself that the conflict isn't about whether you love her. She can confidently tell herself, *He didn't mean it* or *He's just having a bad day,* look past it, and move on.

Whether male or female, all of us need to hear praise in order to subconsciously believe the affirming truth behind it.

6. Honor What They Do Rather Than Focus on What They Don't

Perhaps there are no big problems in the past; instead you're simply dissatisfied. You don't see things worth praising, but you do notice lots of things that aren't what you would like. This usually happens for one reason: skewed comparisons (*Why can't he be more like . . .*) and unrealistic expectations (*If they cared, they would do this*). Most of us have a human tendency to look over the shoulder of the person in our life (spouse, child, colleague), notice a particular trait or factor we admire in someone else, and become dissatisfied with the person standing in front of us. But here's the trap: we are almost always comparing our person's bad stuff to that other person's good stuff.

Perhaps you look longingly at that other family's huge house and become annoyed with your own modest home; you don't see that within those perfectly trellised walls is nasty arguing, frosty silence, addiction, or affairs. Perhaps you envy a different department at the office, where they get every other Friday off; you don't recognize that they have a really harsh boss or that you have very supportive colleagues. Maybe you're jealous of that other student to whom engineering principles come so easily; you don't realize that he or she is jealous of how effortlessly *you* can communicate your thoughts in writing.

There is always something we can praise once we stop comparing and learn to see and appreciate what someone does have to offer (including ourselves!).

One woman I have known for years is the women's ministry director at one of the largest churches in the country. I sat down with her, explained the 30-Day Kindness Challenge, and asked for her feedback. She said,

Wow, you're describing something that happened to me! I always had a good marriage, but I also had this little discontentment. I was focusing too much on the negatives. And one day I was struck by two scriptural truths: First, the command to rejoice always and give thanks in everything. And second, the directive to let every woman respect her *own* husband. I suddenly realized, not only was I comparing my husband and expecting him to be like that other woman's husband, but I was looking only at the other husband's good things and comparing them with my husband's bad.

That day I felt God tell me pretty sternly to appreciate *my* husband and what *he* does. And when I started looking, I started to see more and more that he really is a fantastic husband who takes care of me and our children.

I started telling him how much I appreciate him: "Thanks for taking care of us." "Thanks for taking the kids to the park." "Thanks for showing Joey how to hold the tennis racket correctly." Anything and everything. It changed my perspective. And it changed *him*. He wanted to be better for me. He wanted to do *more*. Respecting and honoring him for who he is revolutionized our entire relationship. It was almost as if I gave him the ability to blossom and flourish, for the greatness that was always there to come out.

Sometimes women will say, "But I don't respect him. So isn't that lying?" No. I am acknowledging what he *is* doing well, even though I'm also hoping he'll rise up to even more of what God is calling him to. We all need to be honored and affirmed for what we are getting right, but in marriage men need it especially. They thrive on it. God gives us the key to their hearts if we'll just do it.

☺ **When we overcome this obstacle and practice praise, we become much more content with what we have.**

Purposeful praise is the antidote to the human tendency to focus on what we *don't* have rather than what we *do*. This is the prescription for becoming happy no matter our situation. And as we become grateful for what others do well, we begin to feel compassion for them, which leads to less critically demanding behavior on our part. (The same outcome occurs, by the way, when we apply this to ourselves, when we try to see what we are doing well rather than what we aren't.)

7. Uplift Others Without Worry of Being Undermined

I received an intense reaction when I told one woman that her relationship with a difficult coworker—a male colleague who, she believed, got better opportunities because of the good-old-boy network—might improve if she found things for which she could sincerely thank or praise him.

"Why should I stoop to that?" she asked, incredulous. "I've been fighting to be seen as an equal player the whole time I've been here. I am good at what I do, and I do not have to stroke someone's ego to get ahead. I'm not playing that game."

It is interesting that many of us see affirmation of others as pandering or as putting us at risk of being diminished in some way. This, too, shows a misunderstanding of the nature of affirmation; in particular in how others view it. Yes, there are certainly those who take affirmation as merely their due. But they are a far smaller slice of the population than many believe. For example, many women believe men have big egos. And yet on every survey I've conducted, at least 75 percent of men have indicated that that ego is just a mask hiding a great deal of insecurity.

Everyone has insecurities. Every human has doubts and worries. So most humans appreciate, and do not take for granted, sincere affirmation.

☺ **When we overcome this obstacle and practice praise, our person thinks more highly of *us*.**

This has been clear in all the years of my research. Whether it is an intimate relationship like that with a spouse or child, or an arm's-length relationship like that with a business client, our choices to express genuine affirmation almost always build gratitude, mutual respect, and affirmation in return. As long as our praise is genuine, our spouses, clients, or bosses view us not as panderers but as those astute enough to see the value in other people and confident enough to say it. We are seen as those who truly care about others, and we are respected as a result.

☐ 8. Compliment Their Way Instead of Trying to Control It Our Way

There's another sneaky reason why some of us don't always give the praise and affirmation others need: we don't even see certain actions as praiseworthy because they aren't done *our* way. Worse, we may even see some actions as deficient when they actually are fine—they just reflect a difference of opinion about method. Not only does being controlling make it unlikely we will praise others' efforts, but it often backfires on us. A wife and mom of three kids put it this way:

Looking for ways to appreciate what my husband does really made me see how controlling I've been by doing everything. Since he works the night shift, I sometimes feel as if I'm a single mom. I do all the shopping, handle the kids, schedule appointments. I haven't really let him do anything. I've always thought he didn't want to, and I thought, *Well, if he's not going to, someone has to!* But I realized I've never backed off and given him an opportunity to do things his way without second-guessing his choices. When we made decisions about the kids, he would give input and without meaning to I would say, "Well, I'm the one who's here all the time, so we're going to do it this way instead of that way." No wonder he backed off. And no wonder I had a hard time at first, finding things to appreciate.

One woman groaned as she described her own light-bulb moment:

I realized exactly why my husband isn't doing much around the house: because I criticize the ways he does things instead of praising him for doing them! Last night, he folded all four loads of laundry and put them away, but he was sort of shoving the clothes into our son's drawers. And I caught myself about half a second before I told him he was doing it wrong! I realized it is *so* not important that he does it the way I would do it, but that he does it. If there's something that truly matters, I can bring it up later. But what he needs at the time is a sincere "thank you."

A man I met while traveling agreed. "If my girlfriend says, 'Thanks, but it should have been done this way,' it's like a stab in the gut. It's the 'no thank you' thank you. I don't know if she realizes that everything she says after the word 'but' cancels out whatever she said before. Yet if she sees something I did and gives me the most basic, sincere thanks, I'm flying!" Many men have told me, "I can hear what needs to change later, but when I make the effort I simply need appreciation."

For many of us, it can be hard to let go enough to recognize when corrections don't matter—to shake off the feeling that affirmation may let someone off the hook. One wife I interviewed came to a sobering realization as her husband began to successfully fight a longtime pornography addiction just as she was starting the 30-Day Kindness Challenge. She said, "For years I've been trying to control the situation, not very successfully. And now he's going to the recovery group, watching the videos he's supposed to watch, and they emphasize that this has to be *his* process and his accountability. I realize, now that I've given him this ultimatum and he's actually done what I asked him to do, I feel completely out of control! I have to give up this idea that the moment I praise him, he'll feel like he can stop."

☺ **When we overcome this obstacle and practice praise, we start to see that their way may be a good way.**
As we force ourselves to let go of our preconceived ideas, we quickly find things to appreciate in the other person's approach and realize that there may be no truly right or wrong approach but just a difference of opinion. And even when there are true mistakes, we will have more grace for them, recognizing that we don't do everything perfectly either.

9. Take Moments to Praise, Even When Your Schedule Is Packed

Even if we don't say, "I'm too busy to focus on this," it's often our subconscious thought. One woman expressed the cry of many a busy mom's heart: "I'm barely keeping my head above water running the kids' activities! Truly, sometimes I just want to drop off my son at soccer, sit in the minivan in the parking lot, and sleep. Or cry. I don't have the emotional energy to focus on finding things to appreciate in my husband." Her words reveal a subconscious assumption that finding things to praise takes energy, takes work. And if that is the case, the next logical stop on the train of thought is to decide that it is something we will need to focus on later. *After tax season. Once school is out. Once things settle down at work. After we get the next budget in. Once my life calms down.*

But life rarely calms down. We don't need to wait for a block of time or energy; we simply need to express a few words at the moment we notice something worth affirming. "That color looks good on you." "Wow, I can't believe you made it on time in that traffic. Thank you." "Great job on that report! I think that will convince them." "You made a good point in the meeting this morning." "I saw you got a 95 on the quiz. Thanks for working so hard, honey."

That's all you need to start. And the outsized impact will make you wonder why you didn't do it before.

☺

When we overcome this obstacle to practice praise, we will see the other person *want* do to more of what led to that great affirmation!

As one man described, "In my previous job, the leadership really didn't think they had time for this sort of thing. It was as if they thought, *We have such limited time and energy. We can't spend it talking about our feelings or building people up.* It was all about efficiency, efficiency—but that efficiency is run by emotional beings! So in terms of results, it made no sense. Of course we don't want to waste time, but if you give me two sentences today to say, 'You did great on this,' I'm going to go bust my tail for the next two weeks. Now *that* is efficiency."

10. Affirm Them in the Little Ways They Need Rather Than Being Stuck on What You Would Need

Finally, one of the greatest roadblocks is also one of the most hidden: we don't know how to praise people in the ways they most want and need. Or because spoken praise doesn't come naturally, we don't do it often enough. This pattern has increasingly greater consequences the more intimate the relationship, often reaching a peak in marriage.

One of the most heartbreaking findings in all my years of research is that most marriage problems are caused not by big issues but by something as tragically silly as a lack of the right information. Usually a husband and wife care about each other (close to 100 percent in our surveys, even among the struggling couples), and they are trying hard. But because each spouse doesn't necessarily understand or recognize the other's (often gender-related or love-language-related) needs and insecurities, they tend to try hard in the wrong areas. A husband pours himself out, giving his wife what he himself would want, and he doesn't realize it has only a minor impact on his mate. And vice versa. Worse, each hurts the other without intending to. So the hurts build, each person becomes convinced the other doesn't care, and the marriage spirals downhill.

The research has been clear that men and women are affected differently by different types of praise and affirmation. Statistically, men are most affirmed by praise that says, "You're good at what you do" and "You're desirable." Women are most affirmed by praise that says, "You're special because of who you are," "You're lovable and beautiful," and "You mean so much to me."

When a wife, girlfriend, or mom notices what a guy does in his day-to-day life and thanks him for it ("Thank you for unloading the dishwasher," "Thank you for always filling up my car with gas"), he finds it more meaningful than hearing, "I love you." In fact, it turns out that "thank you" for a man *is* his version of "I love you." Not surprisingly, sex is also a powerful affirmation for most husbands. We discovered in the study for my book *For Women Only* that for a man, physical intimacy actually meets an emotional need even more than a physical one.

On the other side, when a husband, boyfriend, or dad regularly reassures a woman or a girl of his love and devotion ("I can't believe I get to be married to you," "I love you so much"), tells her how beautiful and special she is, or pauses an emotional argument to give her a big hug, it is a far more meaningful affirmation to her than if he says, "Thank you for always doing the laundry."

The problem, of course, is that it is easy for most women to say "I love you" to their men. It comes naturally! What doesn't come as naturally is noticing their actions and saying "Thank you." What doesn't come as naturally for most women is initiating physical intimacy. Yet both tend to matter far more to men. Conversely, it is easy for most men to say thanks—or initiate sex! What doesn't come as naturally is saying "You are so beautiful" or stepping forward in an argument and giving his wife a reassuring hug. Yet that is usually the type of affirmation she most needs.

We have to retrain ourselves to develop different habits. And those habits go far beyond gender and into other ways of expressing praise—not just the content of the praise but how to deliver it in a way that matters to the other person rather than ourselves.

☺ **When we overcome this obstacle and practice praise, we are more likely to receive what we ourselves need.**

It is astounding the difference that a little new knowledge makes. For more than ten years, our research has consistently revealed this paradox about creating great relationships: when we focus on learning and giving what the other person needs, we are far more likely to receive what we need in the end. Although every situation is different and, sadly, it does not always work this way, I estimate that this paradox succeeds in *at least* 80 to 90 percent of relationships represented by the fifteen thousand men and women we have interviewed and surveyed over the years.

"KILL 'EM WITH KINDNESS"

You've probably heard the great insight attributed to Albert Einstein: the definition of insanity is to do the same thing over and over again and expect a different result. Let's learn that lesson. If we want a person in our lives to do more of what we love and less of what drives us crazy, let's shift away from whatever we are doing now to cajole, criticize, or otherwise try to move them onto a different path. Let's practice praise instead.

I know it can be challenging. One woman described her dysfunctional business environment, and I asked her, "So if you're in that culture, what do you do?" She smiled. "My dad always told me, 'Kill 'em with kindness. Just be kind to someone until you can't be kind anymore. And then be kind some more.' So that's all I can do!"

The question, of course, is *how* we "kill 'em with kindness." Avoiding negativity is one part of the solution. Practicing praise is another. But the third aspect of kindness involves actually *doing* something generous for someone else. Thankfully, accomplishing that is often much simpler than people think. Let's look at this final element of the Kindness Challenge next.

Carry Out Kindness

Eight Types to Try

Element #3 Every day, do a small act of kindness or generosity for your person.

As a child I had a difficult time making friends. I was the kid nobody liked. Although I was desperate to belong, I didn't know how. I talked too much and too loudly. When someone told a story, I jumped in with "Me too," or I had no idea what to say. My concerned parents tried to help and supported my desire to do activities with others—school plays, ballet, service projects—but it often backfired. I was so puzzled why drawing attention to myself didn't make people like me!

Then as I was starting sixth grade, my family went through a terrible tragedy and I lost a family member who was like a big brother—someone who had always loved me for who I was. Overwhelmed by it all, I spiraled into depression and suicidal comments. My parents found a good counselor, which helped with the immediate crisis but couldn't do much about the ongoing reason for my depression: I was an extroverted, friendly kid who didn't know how to make friends.

A year later, while I was on summer vacation at my grandparents' house, my grandfather did something unusual: he handed his unhappy twelve-year-old granddaughter a very old copy of Dale Carnegie's classic book for business leaders, *How to Win Friends and Influence People.* As I read, I was thunderstruck to realize I had been going about it all wrong.

When I got back to school, I pulled out the Carnegie playbook and made a few key changes: Instead of talking about myself, I began to ask others about themselves. Instead of saying "Me too," I asked the next person, "And what about you?" Instead of hanging back when I didn't know what to say, I learned to show genuine curiosity about others. As Carnegie pointed out, when you ask another person to talk about themself ("What did your family do this summer?" "Do you have any pets?" "What's your favorite part about being in the show?"), they will think you are the greatest conversationalist ever!

I found it was all true. People began responding in a completely different way. I'm sure I wasn't totally unselfish and others-focused, but as time passed, I found mature friendships developing for the first time. And today my extroverted heart is happy to have many wonderful friends.

It's All About Generosity

You may wonder what a preteen learning about friendships has to do with kindness. Everything, it turns out. A crucial part of kindness involves putting others first and focusing on them—not on yourself—in acts of generosity. And the truth that my grandfather and Dale Carnegie put me on to is this: even the smallest of those acts of generosity (such as asking people questions about themselves) can change how someone else views you, themself, and your relationship. And that usually translates into more enjoyment for you as well.

You may never have thought of asking someone "What was your summer vacation like?" as an act of kindness before. Join the club! I think our minds immediately go to the random acts of kindness we're used to doing or hearing about. You may have paid for the food for the people in the beat-up car behind you in the drive-through line, brought a friend a cup of coffee without being asked, or given an encouraging card to a colleague who was going through a rough time. And if these types of actions were all we're talking about, it would be easy to assume this kindness thing is nice but doesn't have a big impact unless it is done in volume, with many people taking action at the same time.

But the classic, tangible random acts are only one type of kindness. When I started cataloging the patterns of those who were doing the 30-Day Kindness Challenge, I was amazed to discover that there are *eight types of kindness* that are all meaningful and have a generosity impact. And even the least of these, done regularly, can lead to big changes in the relationship and your enjoyment of it.

In fact, many marriage researchers—including John Gottman, author of the landmark book *Why Marriages Succeed or Fail,* and Brad Wilcox at the University of Virginia—have concluded the same thing I did in my research for *The Surprising Secrets of Highly Happy Marriages*: one key predictor of whether a couple is happy is whether at least one spouse regularly performs small gestures of marital kindness and generosity for the other.[1] These small acts include many of our eight types.

And it doesn't stop with marriage. Whether we are being generous to someone with whom we have a difficult relationship, a person we are close to, an arm's-length colleague at work, or a stranger in the grocery store, simple acts of generosity matter.

NO EXPECTATIONS

There is a caveat: if we want our small acts to positively impact another person, ourselves, and the relationship, we have to perform these acts unconditionally; that is, we have to do them without expecting anything back. I saw this over and over in the research. When we extend an act of kindness expecting appreciation, something being done for us, or even a visible sign that our generosity is having an impact, it will probably backfire, because if we don't see what we're looking for, we easily get impatient or resentful. And either is almost guaranteed to cause worse problems.

As one Kindness Challenge participant told me,

> By far the hardest thing for me was not saying, "Did you see that nice thing I did?" But that is giving to get. The second-hardest thing for me were the weeks when I felt my daughter was just as exasperating as ever and nothing I did was making a smidge of difference. It made me want to stop. But that, of course, is conditional love. And we all know that kindness has to stem from *un*conditional love. Being kind is easy when you feel good and your daughter is a sweetheart and there are no eye-rolls.
>
> We all know true love places no conditions. So you have to ask God for that sort of love, because it is *not* natural. It is supernatural. And when you operate from that place in your heart, you're able to extend kindness whether you feel it or not. It becomes a no-brainer. But you have to pray for God to change your heart first. Then you go in with a true spirit of generosity, and if you happen to see something in return it is an unexpected bonus.

Those of us who take the Bible seriously need to take this unconditional kindness thing seriously too. There's a pretty sobering command in the second letter the apostle Paul wrote to an up-and-coming leader named Timothy: "A servant of the Lord must not quarrel but must be kind to everyone, be able to teach, and be patient with difficult people."[2]

Must be kind to everyone. It doesn't get much blunter than that.

Kindness requires commitment. If you are getting discouraged and thinking, *Nothing I do is ever good enough for her* or *He is never going to change,* check your motivation. And pray! I know how selfish I can be, and like the woman I just quoted, I've had to ask God many times to help me have a pure heart that expects nothing in return. (Thankfully, God delights in answering that sort of prayer. The person we are praying about may be fickle; God is not!)

You also might want to investigate whether you're spending a lot of effort on types of kindness that don't really impact the person you're trying to reach. Just as I mentioned with different types of praise in the previous chapter, various types of kind actions will impact people differently. So keep going, but experiment. Look through one of the versions of *The Five Love Languages* by Gary Chapman to figure out what love language applies to your spouse or child or which language of appreciation applies to your colleague at the office. And if there is a gender divide, I strongly recommend that you take a look at our *For Women Only* and *For Men Only* research to learn more about those hidden things the opposite sex might be longing for.

> ## Question to Consider
>
> When I do something for someone, do I subconsciously (or consciously) expect something in return—and eventually want to stop if I don't get it? If so, how can I come to a place where I extend kindness unconditionally?

HOW TO PRACTICE EIGHT TYPES OF KINDNESS

One pastor summed up the reason for this chapter (and this book!) when she said, "We know we're supposed to be kind, but a lot of us don't really know what to do. Most Christians can quote 1 Corinthians 13, 'Love is patient, love is kind,' but what does that actually mean?"

So let's look at the eight different types of kindness so we can choose what will work best for our lives, our temperaments, and our situations. This chapter could be a whole book of action ideas, but I've summarized the categories below. Bottom line: carrying out kindness means doing a small act of generosity for someone else; overcoming our tendency to be selfish, inattentive, busy, impatient, or focused on our own needs; and doing it without expecting appreciation or anything in return.

My only caution is this: *if possible, do not get stuck on the idea of just doing an act of kindness each day and forget to offer positivity and praise.* All three 30-Day Kindness Challenge elements matter. Remember, following the tip of the day is great as a starting point, but people who sincerely tried to practice all three elements of kindness had a one-third greater chance of improving their relationship.

As before, read this with a pen in hand and check off or make notes about any ideas that (a) you think you most need to work on and (b) you're particularly good at and that might be especially effective. Sure, it's always good to challenge yourself, but be sure to play to your strengths as well! So plan to do those that are a good fit with your ability to be kind to those around you.

1. Perform Small Acts of Service

As I noted, these acts include and even go beyond the traditional random acts that we all tend to think of as kindness. Do the dishes even though it is your spouse's turn. Bring a friend a hot meal and a note when she is stressed. Help a fellow student study, even when your own time is stretched. Gladly change the toner in the office printer even though it's Fred's job. The hallmark here is that the effort is visible; it matters both because of the action itself and because the individual sees that someone cares enough to do that thing for them. Even when the action is anonymous (paying for the order of the next person in line at the drive-through), it sends a tangible message that someone cares.

Most people who participated in the 30-Day Kindness Challenge did it without the other person knowing, either because telling them wouldn't be appropriate (it was for a colleague) or because the action might be discounted ("You're only doing that because you were told to"). Regardless, as one man who did the Kindness Challenge for his wife pointed out, "Even though my wife didn't know I was doing this, she saw that I was making an effort of some kind. Her knowing that was hugely important! In many cases, it was more important to her than the actual things I did. Seeing the intent and effort matters."

In one interview, a mom described her attempts to heal her strained relationship with her grade-school son. For her, nixing the negativity was the most crucial element, but she also found that the little acts of kindness had a big impact. She explained,

> I think some of showing kindness is about surprising him with something he likes. We limit sugar pretty strictly, but out of the blue I made him some hot cocoa. He was so excited! "Mom! You're the best!" It meant so much to him. Such a little thing. I've been really watching to make sure that I am performing kindnesses regardless of how they are received. It takes so little. It didn't take me five minutes to warm water on the stove and make hot cocoa, but to my son, it was as if I roped the moon. Or with my husband, it is as simple as a well-timed "Good job." I think we complicate things like this sometimes.

Another mom told me,

> My son is thirty-six now, but when he was young I used to put notes in his lunchbox—notes that said, "I believe in you," "I love you," and "Thanks for being such a great kid." The other day I was at his house helping him pack because he's moving. In a bottom drawer I came across all these mementos of important things that had happened in his life: an old passport with some special visa stamps, a program from winning a big workplace competition . . . and a little colorful folded note I gave him twenty-five years ago that said, "I'm so proud of you, buddy." I had no idea these casual little notes meant so much to him.

These little acts also matter in the workplace. After all, they are the hallmark of great customer service! One woman told me,

> My daughter Ellie is the sweetest, kindest person you could ever
> know. She worked as a bank teller and would get the most amazing
> gifts at Christmas—which is crazy. Do *you* know your bank teller?
> And yet people would bring her money, doughnuts, CDs, bagels,
> cookies, earrings . . . you wouldn't believe it. And there's one reason:
> she is really kind and helpful to everyone. She is the type of person
> any bank would want on the front lines. When you are in the drive-
> through and have trouble with your ATM card, she doesn't talk you
> through it through the speaker; all of a sudden she's standing by your
> car. And she's so positive. It is very hard to get Ellie to say something
> negative about somebody even if she is furious with him or her. I don't
> know where she came from!
>
> Six weeks ago, she left the bank because someone recruited her
> to sell cell phones. And within six weeks, she was the number two
> salesperson in the state. Why? Not just because she is so kind, but
> because all her bank customers swarmed into her store to buy from
> her! They wanted to help her!
>
> Whenever I hear people say, "Kindness doesn't put food on the
> table," I just roll my eyes. Those people apparently have no idea what
> kindness really means.

☺ **As we do these little acts, we not only make an impact on that person in that moment, but we also send the vital message that someone cares.**
This in turn sends the message, "You're worth caring about. You are important." Every human being wants to feel that way.

2. Give or Share Something Precious to You

Whenever we have something we are reluctant to give or share, it shows kindness when we do just that—especially when we are asking for nothing in return. There are many examples, but here are some I heard most frequently.

Give of your time. This is a big need for most people and is an unrecognized yet powerful type of kindness in almost any relationship. In a workplace focus group, one woman initially objected to the idea of doing the 30-Day Kindness Challenge for her boss because, as she said, "He's married, I'm single, and writing him thank-you notes or bringing him coffee would be inappropriate and send a very wrong message."

Her colleague quickly pointed out, "But kindness is more than that. In my early twenties I was single and had an older male boss, and he went out of his way to show kindness in a completely appropriate way by investing time in training me. He was very busy but was always willing to coach me. I never once felt uncomfortable; he was simply investing in me as a career woman. That was an act of kindness, and here ten years later I'm still thinking about it. So it made an impact."

In addition to workplace relationships, investing time is crucial to making those in our personal lives—partner, children, siblings, and so on—feel cared for. Men, you might find it particularly interesting that in our research with thousands of women for *For Men Only,* 70 percent of married women said, in essence, that if you're losing a lot of time with your wife in order to be sure you can provide for her, she would prefer it the other way around and would even give up financial security if that was what it took to get more of *you.*

In our survey of those who took the 30-Day Kindness Challenge for a romantic partner, nearly eight out of ten people said they improved in this metric: "In general, I tend to drop some personal activities or rearrange what I was planning to do to be more available to my partner." We found that this one factor was a huge predictor of whether they were happier in their relationship and whether the 30-Day Kindness Challenge had improved their relationship overall.

Be More Available, Be More Happy

In general, I tend to drop some personal activities or rearrange what I was planning to do, to be more available to my partner.

	Before	After
Yes I do	46%	73%
Sometimes	29%	21%
Not really	25%	6%

Note: Answers are categorized. See our website for exact wording and analytical details about these results.

Happy in Marriage?

Yes	84%
Sometimes	12%
No	5%

Note: Among those who said they prioritized being more available to their partner.

Give affection. Although this won't matter as much in the workplace, it is something I heard many times in the personal relationships I studied. When we are at odds, affection tends to suffer. We hold ourselves back out of irritation or self-protection. Yet our spouses, our children, or our parents may be longing for it.

Share your home, space, or hospitality. Everyone likes his or her space. So sharing it says something!

Share any item you would like to keep all to yourself. If you have any item you would *not* want to share, then sharing it with someone who would appreciate it is usually a true act of kindness. And not a small one either! I have a few of those types of things I want to hoard: they usually involve sugar. Apparently, I'm not alone.

A friend of ours named Polly makes the best pies I have ever tasted. They are works of art, and I have no idea how she got God himself to touch the pies and make them taste as they surely would have in the Garden of Eden. Unfortunately, they take time to make, so she doesn't produce that many. Receiving one is a rare and precious gift for a very special person—such as the pie she makes for her pastor every Christmas. Last year, in a sermon on generosity, her pastor had to confess that Polly's pies were one way he came to confront his own selfishness: every year he wanted to hide the pie so no one else in the family could eat it! (I know how he feels.)

Maybe for you it is sharing a hard-to-replace tool from your workbench. Maybe it's letting someone borrow your newly purchased car or fragile serving dish for the day. Maybe it is offering the last gourmet chocolate in the jar.

Whatever it is, sharing it speaks care. (Unless, um, the others in the household don't *appreciate* that particular type of chocolate nearly as much as you do, and thus it would be wasted on them. Right?)

Sacrifice some comfort. A couple I'll call Jeremy and Cassie visited friends at a remote mountain cabin for a weekend. Their first evening there, they heard tales of bear sightings in the area. Cassie, who got up each night to let their dog out, suddenly grew nervous at the idea of facing the nighttime wilderness alone. Later that night when the dog whined to go out, Cassie as usual went out with him.

Jeremy told me, "Since we're in a second marriage and want to do it right, I've been praying, *God, let me see right there in the moment when my wife is feeling unloved, rather than three days later when I reflect on it.* That night when I heard our dog whine, I was half-asleep and lying there in that nice warm bed thinking, *Honey, you wanted the dang dog. I didn't, so you can let the dog out!* But then it was as if God quietly said, *You know how you prayed to know when she feels unloved? This is it. She is outside worrying about getting eaten by a bear, feeling as if you don't care.* So I got up. She was coming back in."

Cassie confirmed that she had been outside feeling jumpy and upset that Jeremy hadn't offered to go with her. "But," she said, "as soon as I saw that he had gotten out of bed and was coming to meet me, I saw that he was *willing,* which said he cared. And that was all I needed."

Whenever you sacrifice a little comfort to help someone feel loved, you practice kindness.

☺

As we give up what matters to us—sleep, time, credit, the last piece of our favorite pie—we become more open, less grabby, and more willing to share.

Protecting what we have makes us stingy and closed. When we don't have much or hold what we have loosely, we discover the self-perpetuating joy of being content—and generous—with very little. ABC journalist Jay Schadler put it perfectly in his groundbreaking series *Looking for America.* He hitchhiked across the country and noticed, "Those who had the least were often the most generous with their hearts."[3]

☐ 3. Don't Respond in Kind

If you take the 30-Day Kindness Challenge, you will be trying to not be negative. But what do you do if someone else is negative to *you*? A small act of generosity in this case is not responding in kind. Being gentle, extending grace, forgiving a hurt, and letting something go can be small day-to-day acts of kindness—or really big ones.

This sort of self-control is often one of the hardest things to learn. But it is also one of the most impactful for responding kindly in every area of life. In Psalm 18, King David described a situation in which trouble was everywhere, but because he tried to follow the ways of God, he knew he would survive it well. He made this great comment: "Your right hand upholds me; and Your gentleness makes me great."[4]

Over the years, many impressive leaders have advised that true servant leadership requires having both a soft heart and a thick skin. Although I've tended to have a soft heart, the thick-skin part has taken longer to learn, especially when I read some of the more hurtful, harsh things that others say publicly about me, my family, and my books. Recently, after one of my Patheos.com advice columns replied to a pastor's request for data on a controversial topic, I got this e-mail from someone:

> Wow, Shaunti, you couldn't have been more generic with your answer if you had tried! I'm very disappointed that you didn't mention God or His Word in this, [since His ways] . . . protect us from ourselves and all the sad consequences of our sinful behavior. As soon as I send this off to you, I am unsubscribing from your e-mail list.

Underneath was the person's automated e-mail signature, which included this line from Scripture: "Grace be to you, and peace, from God our Father, and from the Lord Jesus Christ."

I was bristling, fighting a bad cold, and exhausted from this book deadline. When I saw that signature line, everything in me wanted to throw back an e-mail saying, "It is ironic you talk about giving grace!" But *I was writing this chapter!* So I took Lysa TerKeurst's advice (see chapter 6), paused for a few moments to give God a chance to catch up with my anger, then answered, "Thanks for sharing your thoughts. We're so sorry you are disappointed. I wrote the answer that way because the pastor was specifically asking for data. But I do understand that you wish that had been handled differently. We wish you well. Go in peace."

As soon as I pressed send, I actually felt better. If I had responded in kind (as I unfortunately *have* done at other times!), it would have eaten me up. But responding in grace created a lightness of heart.

Many people have consistently found that responding to big hurts with forgiveness has the same effect. This type of generosity sets you free.

☺ **As we carry out these acts of kindness, we start to feel the grace we've decided to show.**

Just as I mentioned in chapter 6 about nixing the negativity, when we say and share agitation, we grow more agitated ourselves. Venting or mouthing off might feel great in the moment, but rarely the next day . . . or even the next hour. Instead, it feeds vindictiveness and tension.

Thankfully, it works the other way as well. Once we refuse to enter into that agitation and instead respond with kindness, not only do we often defuse a tense situation, but we *feel* more kind and peaceful as well.

4. Give Sex

You may have been wondering about this! Or you might be offended at the idea of "giving" sex as an act of marital generosity. Or thinking, *Shouldn't it just be spontaneous?* Alternatively, you may wonder, *Why should it even matter?*

Although every marriage is different, we have seen two relevant truths in our research over the years. First, physical intimacy is crucial for marital happiness (in fact, a 2011 Brad Wilcox study showed it was one of the most critical factors in whether or not a marriage was happy).[5] Second, in many marriages one partner wants significantly more sex than the other. So if the lower-libido partner willingly reaches out to engage in physical intimacy, they are extending a pretty major act of generosity.

And if you are the higher-libido partner, realize: showing kindness often seems to result in this kind of generosity coming back to you! One of the welcome surprises from our surveys came when we looked at those who started the 30-Day Kindness Challenge for a spouse and were not fully satisfied with their sex lives. We looked at that same group thirty days later and discovered that among those who took the actual Challenge, more than half (56 percent) said their sex life improved! And as with every other aspect of kindness, the improvement was present but lower among those who did not do the actual Challenge but focused primarily on the daily tips.

Kindness Is Sexy

"In general, our sexual relationship is satisfying and fulfilling."

	Improved	Declined	No Change
Focused on the three Challenge elements	56%	11%	33%
Focused on the daily tips	31%	25%	44%
Total survey group	**47%**	**16%**	**37%**

Note: Among those who had room for improvement in agreement with the above statement. See more on our website.

All that said, if your sex life is still not what you want it to be, this may indicate you're trying hard in the wrong areas. Now, perhaps your spouse does need some help to get past medical or emotional issues. But it's more likely that one or both of you need to understand some key things about how the opposite sex processes physical intimacy. (If you want a helpful primer, the research in *For Women Only* and *For Men Only* applies to most couples.)

☺ **As we are generous in this way, we realize sex improves not just physical intimacy but emotional tenderness and closeness.**
We'll discover that sex isn't just a physical act but an emotional one. In addition, giving sex improves our actual physical desire. Researchers have discovered that sexual involvement at least once a week raises testosterone levels, which makes the lower-libido spouse (whether male or female) actually want sex more

in the end. By contrast, forgoing sex results in a vicious cycle of lower testosterone levels, less desire for sex, and less sexual activity, and the cycle starts over again. From the many types of research about this topic, it is clear that the decision of the lower-libido spouse to pursue sex is almost always going to yield high returns.[6]

☐ 5. Focus Attention on the Other Person and Be Approachable

Focusing on the other person, not myself, is what I learned to do as a preteen for the first time. And it is a surprisingly powerful little act of generosity or kindness. When you say, "Tell me about yourself," the other person is flattered and feels cared for, appreciated, or important. When you are around others and you draw attention to something good someone else has done ("Guess what? Sarah solved our client problem. Tell them, Sarah."), that person will be loyal to you forever.

Making yourself approachable sends a similar "You are important" message and stands in stark contrast to the notion of acting aloof to impress others. I can still remember the shock of getting fired only two days into a hostess job at the most exclusive restaurant in my college town. "You are too friendly and you smile too much," I was told. "You need to look down your nose a bit. The patrons have to feel that this place is above them and they are lucky to be here." (They must have never read Carnegie.)

This approachable, warm, others-focused character trait also provides a great solution for group dynamics. For example, as leaders of public schools across the country have battled the bullying problem, one school administrator of a large district told us, "We realize that antibullying programs don't really work. We can't effectively solve this by teaching kids to not bully each other. Instead, we have to teach them to be kind to each other. That approach took off like a rocket because that truly is what is needed."

☺

As we carry out this type of kindness, others like and appreciate us more—and we are more grateful for them.

The power pose tells others, "I am oh-so-above you." But when we focus on others, they not only see us as humble and caring, but also, as Carnegie said, they think we're just *spectacular* conversationalists. Which is a win-win, because as one businessman cheerfully put it, "As I learn about you, I usually start to like you more. I appreciate you more. I learn things that will be helpful for the future. But even better, you start to like and respect me. And you think I'm a very astute person, good with people, and so on. All because I got you talking about yourself."

6. Be Fully Present and Enter Their World

Being generous helps us fully enjoy and enter into the moment with someone instead of being distracted and giving someone the impression we'd rather be doing something else. Similarly, generosity helps us step out of our own activities, interests, or way of doing things and step into someone else's. The person may in fact be an interruption to what you need to be doing, but generosity refuses to make them feel like one.

You may have one hundred e-mails screaming for your attention when you get home, but if you want a great relationship with your kids, put down your smartphone for a while and ask about their day. Ditto for your spouse, the person you're meeting for coffee, your assistant who is explaining the boring arrangements for the meeting tomorrow, or your classmate who takes a long time to get to the point. Don't let the urgent crowd out the fun—or the kindness.

As *Washington Post* sports columnist Thomas Boswell said in the Ken Burns *Baseball* documentary, "Life can't be all big issues and heart surgery."

This is a struggle for me. Like everyone else, I have a lot to do. It is difficult to slow down. Literally. When Jeff and I are driving together, even if we're not in a hurry, I'm itching to take the wheel and go faster, weave in and out of traffic to get out from behind those folks who are going *intolerably* slow. But Jeff just looks over at me with a little smile and says, "It's a lot more peaceful when you refuse to be in a hurry and just enjoy the moment." I've learned that my ability to do that is an act of true kindness to him.

It is ironic that many wives mention how much they would love their husbands to put down the video games and talk (guys, we cover this in chapter 9), because one mom told me the reverse was what helped her connect with her third-grade son. He loved playing video games, but whenever he eagerly described the games and their intricacies, she found herself nodding, eyes glazed over.

When I started the 30-Day Kindness Challenge, I finally signed up to play a particular basketball video game on my tablet just so I could understand what on earth he was talking about. This is something he enjoys just as much as if he were playing basketball on a team. It was my little act of kindness to learn to understand it.

I was chaperoning a field trip recently and I heard him bragging to his friends on the field trip, "My mom plays video games with me! Here's what level she is. No other moms play video games, but my mom does."

Playing these video games together has actually become good quality time for us! And honestly, the impact all this has had shocked me. Before I started the Kindness Challenge, he would say these negative things about himself that broke my heart, like "You like Susie [my daughter] more than me." He would get so down on himself and say he wasn't good enough or "I'm so stupid." And that has completely gone away since I started this! Praising him and doing this little thing, playing video games with him, has really helped him feel better about himself.

☺

As we focus on the person in front of us, we are essentially saying, "I value you more than whatever else I could or should be doing."
Perhaps more important, we not only tell them they are worth our time and attention, but we also reinforce that notion to ourselves. As a result, we are far more likely to see even more things we like and appreciate about them that might have gone unnoticed before. And all that makes building a great relationship much, much easier.

7. Assume the Best

One of the most crucial findings from our study of the happiest marriages is this: it is an act of generosity to assume the best of the other person's intentions toward you, even if the evidence suggests otherwise.

Of course we know that other people won't always have great intentions toward us. It would be foolish, for example, to assume that your colleague wants the best for you if she keeps stealing your ideas and presenting them as her own. But contrast that with your spouse or romantic partner. If, for example, he keeps doing something that hurts you, should you assume he is doing it on purpose? Or is it better to assume he is simply having a hard time grasping how something like that feels to you? As I mentioned earlier, close to 100 percent of the married couples we studied—even in difficult marriages—deeply cared about each other. But we all hurt one another from time to time.

The closer the personal or working relationship, the more likely it is that a particular hurt was not intended. So the small act of kindness is this: the next time you're provoked, hurt, shocked, or upset, take a deep breath, assume he didn't intend to upset you, and look for a more generous explanation of his behavior. You will be giving him, yourself, and your relationship a gift.

☺ **As we start to look for more generous explanations, we'll see them often, which will spur us to look for them next time too.**
Soon you'll find that looking for the best and holding back criticism about the worst becomes a habit. A much more helpful one!

8. Tell the Other Person What You Need

One of the greatest traps for many people in relationships is thinking, *I shouldn't have to do this.*

- *I shouldn't have to tell my husband what I want for my birthday—he should just know.*
- *I shouldn't have to tell my wife I'm longing for physical intimacy; she should be as attracted to me as I am to her.*
- *I shouldn't have to tell my mate what kind of help I need with the kids or to wash the dishes, because anyone should be able to see that's what is needed there.*
- *I shouldn't have to remind the kids to brush their teeth, my friend to pick up the carpool on time, or my roommate to set the alarm.*

Even if every one of those statements is true, if you're frustrated it's very possible that you are not sharing what you need. (Of course, it is also possible that you *are* sharing what you expect but that you're expecting something the other person finds difficult or impossible to deliver—a dynamic we cover in *The Surprising Secrets of Highly Happy Marriages*.) As a step of generosity, say something you feel you "shouldn't have to" say and see what transpires. It may sound odd that telling someone what you're expecting is an act of generosity, but if it keeps the other person from experiencing your disappointment, it certainly is.

One woman provided a great example of how she worked through just such an understanding:

During the 30-Day Kindness Challenge, I have learned to ask my husband specifically if I want him to do something like open doors for me, rather than expecting it and then getting irritated if he doesn't. I haven't always been good at that.

One night we were going out on a date—we try to do that once a month—and he was wearing an old T-shirt, shorts, and tennis shoes. I felt deflated. I had carefully selected a nice dress. I did my hair, put on makeup and nice perfume. I was *ready* for a date. When he came in, he could tell something was wrong.

He asked, so I said, "Here's a tip. If you walk the dogs or work out in it, it is not a date-night outfit." I'm sure I could have put it more nicely, but at the moment it was the best I could do. He quickly got up off the couch and changed into a shirt with a collar.

So the next time I was shopping I picked out two shirts on sale and asked him if he liked them. I said, "Here are two new date-night shirts for you." I wish he would have picked them out himself, but he has always been a T-shirt-and-shorts guy. And what's great is he said he appreciated my getting them for him. They really look nice on him and I compliment him when he wears them.

As one woman said, after witnessing a similar change of habit, "A guy is so much happier because he knows how to make you happier—and of course then you're happier too."

☺ **As we tell others what we need, we learn that they usually *want* to do what we want!**

It doesn't always work that way, of course, but especially in close relationships (marriage, siblings, children) it usually does. The people around us care about us and want us to be content, but they don't always know how to please us. Once we share the "how" with them, not only are they better at pleasing us, but we also tend to believe in their positive motives the next time, rather than believing they are doing something only because we asked.

One of the beautiful things about doing these small acts of kindness and generosity regularly is that you suddenly find they are habits. If you figure out two or three of these types of kindness that your person would most respond to and do them, you will be building up kindness competence very seamlessly.

It made me chuckle when I heard this from one husband, a long-distance trucker, who was taking the Kindness Challenge for his wife:

I'm gone a lot, which of course means that Jessica has to do everything solo: get the kids up, make the lunches, send the kids off to school, and so on. So during the Challenge I focused on little acts of kindness like making sure I e-mail her every day to ask what is going on. Or when I was home, I'd be the one to pick up the kids from their activities so she didn't have to.

Well, the Challenge ended last week, and I honestly haven't been focused on all that stuff as much. But yesterday I was home and I woke up before Jessica did, and I just reached over and turned off her alarm since I knew she was exhausted and didn't have to be anywhere that morning.

I got up, made the lunches, and got the kids off to school. About an hour later she came into the kitchen and said, "Oh my gosh! You made the lunches and everything!"

I hadn't even thought about it. That was just the sort of thing that I did throughout the Challenge, but I guess it didn't end when the Challenge ended. It has carried over into new habits and ways of interacting. That's been the biggest plus.

But the other beautiful thing about these habits of kindness is much deeper. When we give kindness, we suddenly become aware of how often we don't. We notice more the kindness that comes to us that we truly don't deserve. And all that gives us an attitude of gratitude that is far more precious than anything we are giving away.

9

A Special Chapter Just for Husbands

An Alternative Element #1

> *Element #1* Don't be distracted and don't withdraw. Give your wife your full attention in conversation for at least fifteen minutes a day. (And when you are upset with each other, stay in the game five minutes past when you want to escape.)

This chapter is for husbands—and any woman peeking in. As we researched the most effective aspects of kindness and how to create a 30-Day Kindness Challenge that would best improve relationships, we discovered something crucial. For one specific subgroup—men doing the Challenge for their wives—the first element of the 30-Day Kindness Challenge (chapter 6) could potentially be counterproductive. Not for every husband, but for some.

As one pastor and marriage counselor reviewed the results of the first few groups to take the Challenge, he said, "These men were doing this to improve their marriages. But when challenged to 'Say nothing negative about your wife,' some of the men said, 'That's easy—I just won't talk,' which really defeated their efforts to improve the marriage! We need to give these particular men an alternative first element of the Challenge."

Another male adviser chuckled when I shared this dilemma: "It only makes sense that the way we communicate kindness to each other would be different for men than for women—everything else is!" His wife, a marriage therapist, nodded. "If a wife is taking the Kindness Challenge for a husband, the first element is perfect since it overcomes that negative tendency to be critical. The key will be to figure out what a guy's negative tendency is so men can challenge themselves to overcome it."

After several months of testing what worked and what didn't, we landed on the best alternative, which stems from one of the main differences between men and women. Guys, you can see more about this and our research on women in *For Men Only,* but here's the main point: If your wife is like most other women, just being married doesn't by itself make her feel certain that you really love her. What makes her secure is a sense of closeness between the two of you. And one of the best ways to build that closeness—in other words, being kind to her in a way that will improve your relationship—is good daily conversation with her during the regular days and reassurance during the bad ones.

But for that to happen, you have to be purposeful about confronting two related and very common tendencies: to be distracted during the regular times and to withdraw during the uncomfortable ones, which is when she most needs that reassurance. Thus, instead of *Don't say anything negative to or about your wife,* the alternative Element #1 for men is this: *Don't be distracted and don't withdraw. Give your wife your full attention in conversation for at least fifteen minutes a day. (And when you are upset with each other, stay in the game five minutes past when you want to escape.)*

Let's take a brief look at how to do that.

Don't Be Distracted: Give Her Fifteen Minutes of Fame

Most women understand that men often need some space and downtime at the end of a long day—after all, women often do too! But after you've had a bit of space, you'll see great benefits in your relationship if you come out of your man cave, put down your smartphone, turn off or walk away from the television or gaming console, and ask your wife something like, "So what happened today?" After she falls over from shock, you will probably see how happy she is to have this time with you.

After he did the husband's version of the 30-Day Kindness Challenge, one man I interviewed provided a great perspective: "I never told my wife I was doing this, because I didn't want her to think, *You're only complimenting me because you have to* or anything like that. But still, after about the first week and a half, out of the blue one day my wife said, 'I really like that when we see each other at the end of the day, you show up and listen. It makes me feel good.'"

Another man who eventually did tell his wife he was taking the Challenge said, "She was excited I was trying something like this." He described a revelation he had along the way:

> I think guys tend to be more hearers than listeners. It's like, "Yeah, yeah, I hear you. I know what you're going to say," and then I want to move on. Once I had to focus on actual *conversation,* I realized I honestly hadn't been giving her that opportunity to fully express herself—to let her talk about what she wanted to talk about—and then truly listen to her.
>
> About a week after the Kindness Challenge ended, I was still trying to practice the elements but wondering whether it mattered. And suddenly she told me, "You know, you've become a really good listener. You let me get my feelings out without having to fix them right away. You seem to want to care about what I care about. I'm really happy when I'm sitting and talking to you." And that blew me away. With that kind of feedback, you bet I'm going to keep this going now!

A Slippery Speaking Slope?

One of the main concerns I heard from men during the initial tests was that the fifteen-minute conversation might open a Pandora's box. As I was talking about this project, one man said, "I know my wife needs to talk, but to be frank, that's one reason I would avoid that 'Give her undistracted attention' thing. I know I don't have the ability to talk about emotional things for two hours, but isn't that what she'll expect if I start this? Once the ball is rolling downhill, how do I stop it without hurting her feelings? I see how she talks and talks with her girlfriends, but I know my brain would freeze and my eyes would glaze over, and then I'd get in bigger trouble."

It's a common concern, but once men try this, they are usually reassured. And when this is in fact an issue, the men in our tests described all sorts of strategies to give the undivided attention their wives needed *and* the realistic time limit they themselves needed. One busy dad described it this way:

> I don't think my wife quite gets that although I love her and want to talk to her, I can do only so much talking before I've used up all my words. I have to let the word bank refill. So I sometimes start a conversation when I know I have just a short time before I have to leave for a meeting or take a shower. I'll say, "Hey, I only have a few minutes before I have to meet Bob, but what happened with Marci today?" If I have to go, sometimes we agree to finish the story when I get back. But a lot of the time, she is totally fine with that concentrated time. She just needs to be able to share what's going on and know that I'm listening.

But What Difference Will Fifteen Minutes Make?

If you don't think fifteen minutes of conversation a day would make a difference—to your wife or to your relationship—think again.

Over the years, many men have told me that one of the most uncomfortable, frustrating experiences for a guy is the sense of being confused by his wife's feelings. Many guys who took the 30-Day Kindness Challenge told me that before they started, confusion was a regular occurrence. And yet 83 percent of the men said they better understood their wives just thirty short days later!

In particular, when I looked at the group of men who had paid the most attention to this alternative element, only 39 percent started out feeling confident that they understood their wives' feelings. Yet by the time the Challenge was over, that number nearly doubled, rising to 72 percent!

Furthermore, these men were more likely to end up with greater enjoyment in marriage, a better sex life, and feeling more appreciated than the average participant.

Listening may seem like a little thing, but it sure has an outsized impact.

A Little Bit of Listening, a Lot Less Confusion

Among men who gave their wives fifteen minutes of undivided attention four or more times per week.

"I generally understand my partner's feelings."

	Before Challenge	After Challenge
Strongly/moderately agree	39%	72%
Slightly agree	22%	0%
Slightly disagree	11%	22%
Strongly/moderately disagree	28%	6%
Total	**100%**	**100%**

Just Make Sure You're Listening to Her Feelings

After doing the previous research with my husband, Jeff, I have only one caution: guys, make sure you're using those fifteen minutes to listen *in the way she'll feel listened to*. One man described the common trap men tend to fall into, explaining, "As a guy you want to fix it and you don't want to sit and listen. So our response is, 'But what do you want me to *do* about it? I love you, so what can I *do* for you? I want to go kill some meat and feed our family.' We want to provide and protect, and listening seems so passive for us. But I know it is active for women—we just need to see it that way."

Yes, it is active for us women. Here's the bottom line from the *For Men Only* research: to your wife, *listening* means "listen to how I'm *feeling* about what I'm sharing, not the problem itself."

I know that sounds weird. But it works. Investigate all those emotions you might normally want to avoid ("Did what Marci said hurt your feelings?"). Ask what so-and-so did in response. Pull out what your wife thought and felt about it all. You can get to the "What do we do about this?" step later. But if you start with listening to her feelings, your wife will feel heard.

And Make Sure You're Undistracted . . .

Your wife won't feel listened to if you're glancing at your phone during that fifteen minutes. But when you purposefully demonstrate that you're giving her your undivided attention, it really matters. Look how one woman who had done the 30-Day Kindness Challenge for her husband described her feelings when she saw that dynamic unfold:

> My husband has his phone or iPad in his hand almost constantly. I don't think he realizes he is sending me a signal that says, *I don't really care about you being here or what you're saying.* It's a bit painful, actually. We even went away for the weekend, got a "romance package" with a beach-front room, champagne, and chocolate-covered strawberries. And as I uncorked the champagne and handed him a glass, I saw he was playing solitaire on his phone! Seriously?
>
> I took a sip and thought for a second about how to handle it. I didn't ask him to put the phone away, give him the silent treatment, or think, *Well, there goes our "romantic getaway,"* the way I might have a month ago. Instead I said what a romantic place it was and how yummy the strawberries were and that I loved him.

He looked up at me, put the phone right down on the table, and leaned over and gave me a kiss. Score one for kindness. And for the rest of the weekend, I could actually tell he was *there* with me, instead of his body being there but his brain a hundred miles away with his colleagues. It was an amazing feeling.

. . . Or Tell Her When You Will Be

One woman told me of a success strategy her husband discovered: if you can't give your wife your attention right then, tell her when you'll be able to.

I recognized that Isaac had work to do or there were things he enjoyed and wanted to do to unwind after a long day. But I got so frustrated because I didn't have any idea how long he'd be playing basketball with the guys or writing up his report. It started to cause some nagging, headaches, and avoidance, which drove both of us crazy. So we came up with an idea. He would tell me—or sometimes I would ask—how much longer until he wrapped up. Once I had a time frame in mind, it didn't seem endless.

The hard part is that when a husband plops down and plays video games or goes and sits at his desk, his wife has no idea whether it will be ten minutes or past midnight. And it really speaks to a woman's heart when the guy says something like, "I'm going to take one hour to finish this project, and then we'll play with the kids."

DON'T WITHDRAW WHEN EMOTIONS RUN HIGH

If you're like most men, when you are upset with your wife or she is upset with you, you probably want and need some space. But if your wife is like most women, your act of pulling away triggers a subconscious *Does he really love me?* insecurity. And it is quite painful. The uneasy question *Are we okay?* circles around in her heart until she is reassured. One woman I interviewed described the sensation well: "I try to focus on whatever else I'm doing that day, but to be honest, nothing is right with the world until that is resolved."

Another woman said, "I don't think guys know how scary male anger can be. When I do something that makes him feel criticized or like I don't trust him, he sometimes gets so mad he has to leave the room before we've worked it out. Men need to know how hard that is for women. I know guys think it is illogical, but the feeling we have is, *This is the beginning of things going bad.* It is an awful feeling."

What's the solution? Instead of escaping, hang in there for a few more minutes. And when you do need to withdraw, reassure her by saying, "I need some space to think, but I want you to know we're okay." On our *For Men Only* survey, between 86 and 95 percent of women said those steps would diminish or solve their turmoil. (One quick caution: Know thyself. Hanging in there a bit longer often provides the reassurance a wife needs. But if you know that in your anger you are going to say or do something that will upset her *more*, then be wise, say, "We're okay," and take a time-out.)

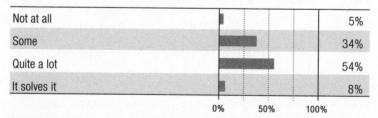

Reassurance Works

In an emotional conflict, if your husband / significant other initiates a step to reassure you of his love, how much does it help diminish any turmoil you are feeling? (Choose one answer.)

Not at all	5%
Some	34%
Quite a lot	54%
It solves it	8%

0%   50%   100%

Note: Because of rounding, results slightly exceed 100 percent. Originally published in *For Men Only*. See *For Men Only* and our website for a description of the methodology and study group involved in this study.

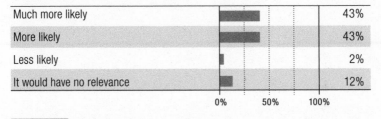

"We're Okay" Works Even Better

Suppose you and your husband / significant other are in the middle of an emotional conflict, and he eventually says, "I don't want to talk about this right now." If he were to add a reassurance such as, "I want you to know that we're okay," would that make you more or less likely to be able to give him space? (Choose one answer.)

Much more likely	43%
More likely	43%
Less likely	2%
It would have no relevance	12%

0%   50%   100%

Note: Originally published in *For Men Only*. See *For Men Only* and our website for a description of the methodology and study group involved in this study.

YOU'LL SEE THE DIFFERENCE!

Only you can decide whether the original first element (say nothing negative) or this alternative is more crucial for your relationship. Certainly, this alternative has proven to be effective for men in their marriages. It requires a little more attention on your part, but it is also likely to yield much richer dividends over time.

Why? Long after the 30-Day Kindness Challenge is past, these particular actions will yield deep benefits in your relationship if they become a genuine habit. So rustle up the routine! Practice these things during the 30-Day Kindness Challenge and watch what happens.

10

Ready, Set, Change

Kindness for Life

N ot long ago, the CEO of a major company was introducing me and one of my business partners as we were about to speak at the company's annual convention. We were helping this corporation create an initiative that would advance more women into leadership. They needed this because they couldn't grow without innovation, and with 95 percent of their executives being male, they couldn't innovate without more variety of thought at the top. The CEO acknowledged that doing things differently would take effort and attention but then flashed these words up on the screen as we took the stage:

> *Nothing changes if nothing changes.*

I told him later that I needed to borrow that phrase. It sums up the perspective that every one of us needs as we look at the improvements we want in our relationships, our lives, and our culture.

Kindness has to start somewhere before it can spread. Change starts with you, the person holding this book. If you want a more enjoyable home or work life, if you want to feel more loved and appreciated by some other person, the first move rests entirely with you.

So take stock of what you can change, what you can work on in order to live a lifestyle of kindness. Go through the self-assessments and the various other assessments and tools online at JoinTheKindnessChallenge.com. Do the 30-Day Kindness Challenge (you can sign up for daily reminders online or use those in the Toolbox section). Try to find and fix your blind spots, your lack of kindness, your areas of negativity. Build a habit of daily praise. Implement the types of generosity that you know, deep down, are needed. And do it all regardless of whether others do the same. Your personal commitment to be kind will change everything in your life for the long run.

One woman submitted this profound comment after she completed the 30-Day Kindness Challenge for her husband:

> My eyes have opened. Over twenty years of marriage, I really believe
> most of the issues we were having stemmed from me and my view of
> our relationship, my reactions to situations, some misunderstandings,
> and simply not knowing what mattered to my husband—such as how
> much he needed my respect. I am now learning to do what matters.
> I'm trying to get over conflicts more quickly, not take everything so
> seriously, relax, stop wishing he would change, and accept him as a
> whole and wonderful person. I am nowhere near perfect—why should
> he be? I have asked God to change me instead.
>
> It's a great start. And I am so blessed. I know my husband loves
> me, although I think many times I have been hard to love. I just needed
> a change . . . an attitude of gratitude. Thankfully, I'm on my way now.

So get on your way . . . then don't give up. As you can tell from the preceding chapters, one of the beautiful things about kindness is that it changes your heart toward the other person so that you *want* to keep being kind. This is especially crucial if you don't see any impact of your actions in the short term.

I am always distressed when I see people drop out of the 30-Day Kindness Challenge after a few days or a week or two. Often their main reason for stopping is something like "I didn't see a difference" or "You would think I would get a better response."

After a few days? After two weeks? Most of us are creating new patterns to replace those years in the making! Healing broken marriages, transforming contentious working or school relationships, eliminating tension with in-laws, reaching the heart of a child who has become closed and withdrawn . . . None of those can be expected to change in two weeks, or even thirty days.

Now, sometimes we do see dramatic changes that quickly—often, even. But sometimes the seed of kindness needs to be planted, watered, and tended carefully over several seasons before it grows and blossoms into the beautiful thing we are longing for.

Sometimes the main benefit of the 30-Day Kindness Challenge is that it builds crucial habits for the long term.

So build the habit.

Then build the lifestyle.

Don't give up.

How to Persevere

You may rightly ask how to *not* give up when the hard moments come, when the 30-Day Kindness Challenge gets especially hard, or when the Challenge is months past and you really, *really* want to revert to your "pre-kindness" self.

There are many success strategies for perseverance over the long run, but here are three good examples to keep in mind as we wrap up our journey together.

Success Strategy #1: Look for Things to Be Grateful For

The Roman philosopher Cicero wrote, "Gratitude is not only the greatest of virtues, but the parent of all others." And much research over the years (including my own) has confirmed just how true that is.

One woman did the 30-Day Kindness Challenge to improve a shaky relationship with her son. When she completed the Challenge and her relationship was so much better, she described her revelation about what was central to the whole effort's success:

> I realized that so many of the problems that bugged the stew out of me were things that my own reactions had caused. I realized that this kindness thing might have a lot to do with climbing out of the pit that I dug myself and voluntarily sat in. It has so much to do with looking around and really *seeing* and being grateful for what you have, rather than being whiny about what you don't. It makes so much sense. And there's almost no way to be kind and others-focused and to respond well *without* that sense of thankfulness for what the other person offers us.
>
> And there's almost no way to have that thankfulness without allowing God to open your eyes to it. Gratitude happens when we see how much we don't deserve anything and how much God gives us anyway. Or when we realize we've hurt him or someone else so badly, or been so selfish, and we are so grateful to be forgiven. Once we realize we don't deserve kindness and get it anyway, it frees us up to give kindness whether or not someone deserves it. And I honestly think that is *the thing* that has to happen if we are to truly be transformed, generous people whose lives are marked by kindness.

Success Strategy #2: Catalog the Encouraging Signals You Are Watching For

In addition to cultivating an attitude of gratitude, we can take practical actions as well. Although we certainly need to track all the results of our efforts, we can particularly fuel perseverance by noticing, cataloging, and reminding ourselves of every positive result as we go. We human beings apparently have weird memory circuits that easily remember the negative and forget the positive.

That's one reason we need to keep a journal or notebook as we go through the 30-Day Kindness Challenge: to capture any encouraging signals, answers to prayer, or good results that we'll otherwise lose sight of over time.

Reminding ourselves of those results keeps us going. When we asked one woman if anything had changed for her and her husband after the 30-Day Kindness Challenge, she initially wasn't sure. She had to ponder the question for a moment. Then she said,

> Yes, I think so. Well, for one thing, I'm more attuned to the power of
> my words and the impact they have on my husband. I'm more willing
> to acknowledge and respect and even appreciate the differences in how
> we express and show our love for each other. I make it a point every day
> to do or say something that encourages him. That's definitely a change.

As she continued to ponder, more started coming to her mind—things she either hadn't ever consciously cataloged or hadn't reminded herself of for a while.

> And now that I think about it, my husband has absolutely amazed me.
> He is more thoughtful, kind, and communicative, and he talks about
> deep things, not surface stuff. He has showered me with little gifts just
> because he loves me. He has been intentional about following up on
> promises he has made. He laughs more, and so do I. I guess more has
> changed than I realized!

Success Strategy #3: Celebrate the Responses You Are Hoping For

Although our focus needs to be on what *we* can do, when the people in our lives respond, we do need to give positive feedback so they are encouraged to keep going!

Many people who take the 30-Day Kindness Challenge choose to not tell the other person they are doing it. But one man told us that he told his wife *because* he knew she would encourage him, and he wanted to make sure he got that positive feedback! He then made a helpful point:

> Throughout the Challenge, Carrie would give me feedback immediately: "Thanks so much for doing that," "I noticed you did that good thing." That feedback provided in a relatively short order is what helped me keep going. For guys, at least, encouragement makes you stick out your chest and say, "Awesome." It's as if we're so glad the other person noticed and appreciated it that now we want to do it even more.
>
> If a wife doesn't give that feedback and gratitude, she is going to miss out on seeing change in her mate. But when she does, man, what guy doesn't want to hear that gratefulness from his wife? And because she's so good at it, I've been continuing even now that the Challenge is over! It isn't just that after a certain number of days it became a habit, but because I've been getting this kind of feedback.

CHANGED HEART, CHANGED LIFE

So what happens when the thirty days are over? That is when real life begins. But let me encourage you: The movement doesn't have to stop. The habits don't have to wane!

I caught up with one man four months after he had finished the 30-Day Kindness Challenge. He had used the alternative first element for husbands, trying to do the "listening thing," as he described it. He had a great perspective:

> Apparently I wasn't all that good at this beforehand. So this challenge was hugely beneficial. The best part is that it has been a lasting change.
> I think like a lot of guys, I had a temptation to check the box—to

just do this each day to cross it off my list. And the risk is that when the Challenge ends, we think, *Hey, we're done,* and then we go back to turning on the ballgame and doing whatever.

But I found that every day, stopping to have a conversation with my wife became a little more automatic and easier for me. It became less and less of a thought process. Also, after a while I realized I didn't have to purposefully remember to affirm her. I just do it now. I don't have to think about any of it, really. I got past the habit-forming part, and these truly are habits now.

And she has clearly appreciated it in a big way. She is so much happier with that purposeful daily check-in. That is huge. I have told some other guys about the Challenge because it is worth every bit of effort to get these results.

As his comments imply, so much of what changes in us is simple awareness, which allows us to see the fruits of our labors and encourages us to be purposeful over the long term. Let's have the same resolve as the woman who told us, "This Challenge came at the perfect time. I knew I needed to change and this helped me get started. My eyes are now open and I don't plan to ever close them again."

As you move forward, don't just look for opportunities to be kind; keep your eyes open for what happens when you are—over both the short term and the long haul. Because the results you get, in both your relationships and in yourself, will be the best possible incentive to continue.

Let me close with this great quote from someone who had started off with an extremely difficult relationship and saw what happened when she simply applied the three elements of kindness:

I learned a lot about myself. I had to daily die to self and choose to be kind. As I did, my eyes were opened to see the goodness in the people

I'm doing this for. And I loved seeing the stress and tenseness literally drop from their faces. I came to realize that praise, affirmation, and generosity aren't that hard. I came to realize that being negative and nitpicking take way too much energy.

In the end, it just feels better to be kind.

Part III

Thirty Days of

Kindness Tips

R eady to jump into the 30-Day Kindness Challenge? You can anony-mously sign up at JoinTheKindnessChallenge.com for thirty days of re-minders, optional ideas for each day, links to assessments (including our printable Self-Assessment Action Plan), helpful articles, and other resources. Or simply come back to this section of the book each day. (Note: These daily tips are not exactly the same as those you would receive through e-mail.) Here, you'll see three versions to choose from, tailored for the following:

- A *wife* doing the Challenge for her husband.

- A *husband* doing the Challenge for his wife.

- Any *person* doing the Challenge for anyone else. This general version is for those who want to do the Challenge for a child, colleague, romantic partner, in-law, classmate, parent, neigh-bor, and so on. (On our website you will find a few additional specialized versions.)

A FEW PRACTICAL SUGGESTIONS BEFORE YOU START

- To get the best results, be sure you focus on doing the three elements of the Challenge, whether or not you use any of the daily tips.
- As you go, keep in mind what you have identified from reading this book that you most need to work on.
- Take the pre-assessment at JoinTheKindnessChallenge.com to better understand *your* kindness quotient.
- In your journal or notebook, document what you try each day and what you see as a result.
- Consider creating a gift journal: write down your Element #2 affirmations each day in a separate journal and give it as a meaningful present on or after Day 30.
- For support and accountability, grab a friend or four to do the Challenge with you. Share your journey on your blog or social media to encourage others doing the Challenge as well.

Now pick the version of the 30-Day Kindness Challenge that applies to you and get started!

Doing the Challenge for Your Husband

Ladies, here's your challenge. For the next thirty days:

1. Don't say anything negative about your husband (either to him or about him to someone else!).
2. Each day find one thing you can praise or affirm, and tell both him and someone else.
3. Each day do one small act of kindness or generosity for him.

Day 1: *The Challenge Begins Today!*

And weeee're off! Today, do something out of the ordinary for your husband, something you think he would enjoy. For example, is there something you used to do for him but have stopped doing as you have gotten busier? Maybe make the run to the dry cleaner for him, take him a surprise lunch at work, or even pull some lingerie out of the back of the closet to surprise him tonight. Write a sticky note related to the surprise action that says "Because I love you" and put it somewhere he'll see it.

Day 2: *Think on the Past*

What character trait did you most appreciate about your husband when you first met him? How does that thing you loved back then tend to show up now? Tell your husband about it: bring up a story and explicitly say what you appreciated then and enjoy now.

If that character trait doesn't still show up (hey, we all slow down and get busy), simply reminisce about that story and how that trait attracted you to him. Make sure you tell the story in a reflective, admiring way, with no wistfulness. Otherwise, he will hear the negative tone asking, *Why don't you do this anymore?*

Note: If you want to make a gift journal, remember to start it today! (Each day write something different that you are thankful for and really appreciate about your husband. Then give him your journal once the Challenge is done. It's a spectacular present!)

Day 3: Leave a Note

Where can you leave a quick note of recognition for something your husband recently accomplished? Maybe it was a particular achievement at work. ("So proud of you for hanging in there even though that customer was so difficult.") Maybe it was a fitness or weight goal met or a home project started. ("I *love* how the bookcases are looking!")

Whatever it is, your recognition will make him fly. Seven in ten men on our surveys said it deeply pleases them when their wives say things like, "You did a great job at that."

Our bet: he's going to keep that note.

Day 4: Brew Up Some Love

Bring your husband his morning coffee just how he likes it. Or make him that protein shake he always chugs in the morning, even if you've never dared try to figure out that concoction before.

If you aren't sure exactly how he makes up his morning brew (whatever it is), watch closely this morning or some other morning soon, and then make a note to do this act of kindness the next day.

Even better, when you surprise him by handing him his morning joe, mention something he has done for you recently. ("You always get me my oatmeal in the morning, after all . . .")

Day 5: Stop, Think, Praise Your Man

Today, replace *Why doesn't he ever . . . ?* thoughts, which are often unrealistic, with thoughts that answer the question: *What* does *he do that makes me feel special, valued, or loved?*

Then tell him what he does that makes you feel special—in a text, e-mail, phone call, or in person. For example:

- "I was just thinking about how you stood up for me in that awkward meeting at church. Thanks for believing in me."
- "I love how you always reach out and take my hand when we're walking. It makes me feel special."
- "You always hold the door open for me. I really love that."

Try it! We bet you'll be shocked at how such a little bit of recognition makes him light up! (Hint: it isn't little to him.)

Day 6: Thank You = I Love You (to Him)

What did your husband do today that you can thank him for? Text, e-mail, phone, and face to face all work! ("Thanks for replacing those burned-out light bulbs before you left." "Thanks for driving the kids to school.")

If you're creating the gift journal, make sure you write a note of thanks in it.

Tip: Don't think "thank you" matters that much? You couldn't be more wrong! In our surveys, 72 percent of all men said it deeply pleases them when their wives notice their effort and sincerely thank them for it. Believe it or not, "thank you" is man-speak for "I love you." (See more in chapter 2 of *For Women Only*.)

Day 7: Think on the Positive When Feeling Negative

Accountability check: Has your husband done anything in the last few days that has really frustrated or hurt you? How did you handle it? Did you force yourself to look at the good things he has done? Did you share your words of affirmation with him just as on all normal days?

—OR—

Did you . . .

- Share your frustration with someone else? (Understandable, but a habit we're trying to break with this Challenge.)

- Find yourself making your existing concern even bigger in your mind? (*And he also does this . . . and this . . .*)
- Have difficulty letting it go?

In your personal journal, make note of how you've been able to do well, how he responded, and what you most need to work on.

Note: If you want a personalized assessment of how you're doing so far and what you most need to work on, take one of our quizzes at JoinTheKindnessChallenge.com.

Day 8: Put a Smile on His Face . . . in a Way Only You Can

Send a sexually flirtatious message to your husband today. We guarantee it will put a private smile on his face, no matter who is around when he reads it!

Then, of course, be sure to follow through tonight! In our surveys, 85 percent of all men said they are deeply pleased when their wives show that they desire them and are pleased sexually. And when you flirt and are sexually playful, you tell him not only that he is desirable to you but also that you care about him and like being with him in that way. If your husband is like most men, all those things will be very meaningful to him.

Day 9: From Work World to Personal World, Help Him Transition

When you and your husband walk in from work, school, or whatever else you've been doing today (or during the workweek, if today is a weekend day for you), make a specific effort to give your husband some downtime to shift from Work World into Personal World. Maybe even bring him something to drink while he relaxes, with no pressure to talk. (Or if he was the one at home today, take over domestic duties for a few minutes so he can have some downtime.)

Later (for example, over dinner), ask him about something he is proud of that you might not yet know about. For example: ask him what the best thing was about his work today or what he feels the proudest of in the last few weeks. Then join in his excitement, no matter what he shares.

Tip: Sometimes men don't like to talk about work because they feel their wives will second-guess what they did. ("Well, if you felt your boss didn't realize XYZ, why didn't you tell him?") And they sure don't want to talk about what didn't go well because they are already feeling inadequate. But if they know they can share an accomplishment or a memory and their wives will be truly excited for or proud of them, they'll chatter all night! (Okay, that's a slight exaggeration. But you get the idea.)

Day 10: Couples Who Do This Are Five Times More Likely to Be Happy

Spontaneity test! Take your husband out for ice cream.

Couples who spend some time together talking or sharing an activity at least once a week are five times more likely to be "very happy" than those who don't. (What a great excuse to run out for ice cream, don't you think?)

Leave the kids at home or with a neighbor for this quick outing so that it's just you and him. And the ice cream.

Day 11: Recognize the Big Stuff

Think about one of the bigger chores your husband does regularly (for example, mowing the lawn and clipping the hedges) and what it would be like if you had to do it instead. Then thank your husband for doing it.

For extra value, brag on him for his consistent work on that chore in front of someone else, such as your mother, a neighbor, or one of his friends. ("Yeah, it was hot yesterday and Jerry was out there digging up the ugly bushes for me. So sweet of him.")

Tip: Notice the next few times your husband does that same task and express appreciation then too. It will help you see all sorts of things you may not have noticed before. When we talk to women who have lost their husbands, we frequently hear them say they had no idea how much they relied on their husband to do certain things. Thankfully, with greater awareness, we can learn that lesson without the pain of loss!

Day 12: *How to Handle Unrealistic Expectations*

Are there things you wish your husband did but you feel that if you have to tell him it doesn't count? Or do you ever think, *If he really loved me, he should be able to do such and such?*

Today, identify a few expectations. They're likely to be the things that cause conflict, leaving you disappointed and him angry.

Next, recognize that if your husband is like the vast majority, he wants to make you happy but sometimes finds it difficult or impossible to meet certain expectations. Identifying where an expectation might be a bit unrealistic is vital. (On our survey for *The Surprising Secrets of Highly Happy Marriages,* one reason the happiest couples were so happy was that they were twelve times more likely to say they didn't allow themselves to hold those unrealistic expectations to begin with.)

So today, pick just one expectation that might be unrealistic (even if it seems that it should be easy!) and that you can let go. Tell your husband you know he wants to make you happy, and apologize if you have unintentionally made him feel like a failure. Then tell him you want to let go of that particular issue, and in your personal journal write down ways you can make that happen.

Day 13: *A Picture Is Worth a Thousand Words*

Look back through the pictures you've taken, whether from last week or thirty years ago, and choose one that reminds you of a great time you and your husband spent together—a time that he made very special in some way.

Print out a copy of the picture (or make a copy of the old photograph) and leave him a note with the picture that recalls your memory of appreciation. ("Look what I found. I was thinking about that river rafting trip. I was so scared and yet you kept telling me I could do it. Thanks for always believing in me.")

If you are making a gift journal, be sure to put that story (and maybe a copy of the picture) in the journal.

Day 14: Admire His Parenting Skills

If you have kids or stepkids, consider: What does your husband do as a dad than you do as a mom? It could be something he does differently because he is a dad, including the stuff that might make you wince.

For example, does he push your toddler daughter on the swing harder than you would like? Does he wrestle your preteen son with so much gusto he risks breaking the furniture? Does he take a different type of disciplinary stand with your teenager than you would? Or if your kids are long grown and gone, does he spend a lot of his time with your adult son talking about football and only a little time talking about the thorny problem your son is facing at work?

Today, instead of wishing he would handle something more like you, tell him how much you appreciate and trust the way he does handle it.

If possible, even catch your husband doing something great with the kids today and point that out as an example. ("You know, it scares me to death how hard you guys wrestle, but I love that you love getting in there and doing that with him.")

Day 15: Two-Week Status Check

How are you doing with the 30-Day Kindness Challenge? Have you been able to avoid being negative? Has your husband said anything about your efforts or given any positive affirmation? Have you noticed anything about his responses that has encouraged you? And have you noticed any differences in yourself?

Get out your personal journal today and record your thoughts. Make special note of the things that seemed to mean a lot to him and those things that helped you respond to him well. What is working, and what do you want to do differently? Perhaps take one of the assessments at JoinTheKindnessChallenge.com to take stock.

If the two of you are doing the Challenge together, this is a great time to stop and talk about it. What does he say means the most to him? What matters the most to you about your husband's efforts?

Regardless, remember that the Challenge is not about getting recognition for your efforts but about developing some good new habits in how you think, speak, and act. If your husband is responding in a pleasantly surprised sort of way, great! But if he isn't responding the way you had anticipated, don't give up. These habits will serve you well for the rest of your life. Keep it up!

Day 16: *The Best Kind of Surprise*

Tonight at bedtime, give your husband the best kind of surprise. Play footsie with him under the covers, put on an intimate outfit, or do something else that signals that you are approaching him for a little one-on-one intimate time. Then enjoy the evening!

Note: Although the majority of men tend to want sex a bit more frequently than women, that desire isn't universal. On our surveys and the various studies on this subject, somewhere between 10 and 20 percent of couples were flipped, with the wife having the greater desire for physical intimacy. If that applies to you, search for the article "When She Has the Stronger Sex Drive" on Shaunti.com and consider how you might respond given how your husband is wired.

Day 17: *Tell Him What You Like*

What is one thing your husband does or says that makes you feel special? Maybe it is little: he tells you you're beautiful, or he puts his arm around you when you're watching TV. Or maybe it is big: he supports your time-consuming volunteer leadership with the animal-rescue league, including the fact that you bring home all sorts of critters, even though animals really aren't his thing.

Whatever that thing is, tell your husband and thank him for doing it. (If you're keeping a gift journal, be sure to note it!)

Ladies, it may feel uncomfortable to tell your husband something like, "I love it when you tell me I'm beautiful." But it's likely that he truly doesn't realize it matters so much to you. Since he wants to make you feel special, it is vital to let him know what works. And then when he does it again, reinforce it by letting him know how great it makes you feel.

Day 18: Get the Kids Involved

If you have children, what can you do to help your children appreciate your husband more? Today, bring up those things he does and explicitly make the connection for your kids that this is a big way he shows how much he loves them. ("I know Dad / your stepfather has to travel for his job, but he doesn't want to be away from you. In fact, he's working hard so that we can enjoy this house and pay for your soccer league. Working hard for us is one of the big ways he says, 'I love you.'")

Then ask your kids how *they* can show their appreciation for him today. Ideas could include giving Dad a neck rub, getting him a bowl of ice cream, drawing a picture for him, or doing one of his chores, like taking out the trash or cutting the grass. If they are older they might call him to catch up.

And if you're creating the gift journal, have your kids write an appreciative note in it to your husband. (Even if your kids are grown and gone, get them to e-mail that note, then print it out and tape it into the journal.)

Day 19: Brag About Him

Brag on him in public. That's right. The men in the research said they'd be flying high if they knew their wives just *happened* to mention something that they did well.

Today, or in the next few days, figure out a natural way to mention to someone else a great comment about something he did. Be specific.

Did he do something particularly great with your kids recently, such as make a good connection with your son on a scout trip? Tell your girlfriends at the office.

Can he repair or build almost anything in your house? Tell the other couple, out at dinner, about how much money he saved by installing the kids' swing set himself.

Did he recently accomplish a fitness goal? Share that with your friends in your book club.

Note: *He doesn't have to be with you* for this to matter. And if he isn't, then tonight oh-so-casually tell him, "I was talking to the girls at the office about the scouting trip and told them how great you were with the boys." Watch his eyes light up!

Day 20: Your Confidence Boost Makes a Difference

What challenges or expectations is your husband facing in the next week or so at work? If today is a workday for him, before he leaves, think of something you can say or text to him that will let him know you have confidence in his ability to rise to whatever expectations or challenges he has to meet.

Oh, and by the way, when he feels like he's providing satisfaction for you in the bedroom, it gives him confidence in the boardroom. There is nothing wrong or manipulative about using this knowledge strategically. When you know your husband has a very important test or meeting coming up, you have an opportunity to significantly influence his sense of confidence the night before that meeting. If you initiate sex with him and let him know clearly how much pleasure he is able to bring you, he will go off to that challenge the next day feeling as if he's on top of the world—and the top of his game.

Day 21: How Does He Make You Happy?

You've heard that guys are performance oriented, right? That mainly means they are focused on trying to *do* things that matter, and most husbands are particularly focused on trying to do things that will make their wives happy. So today, be on the lookout for something your husband says or does that you can tell (once you're looking for it) is an attempt to make you happy. Then acknowledge it.

In our surveys, 88 percent of husbands said they were deeply pleased when their wives made it clear they made them happy (a big smile, words, a hug). So when your man does something that pleases you today, be sure to express that happiness to him. And be specific! ("It made me so happy when I saw you helping Peter with his homework and not getting frustrated even though he was. I love how you handle our kids.")

Day 22: Take a Walk

Get some fresh air with your husband and take a hike together or just a long walk in your neighborhood.

Tell him what you enjoy most about just hanging out with him. Does it make you feel young again? Do you love the fact that you two have time to talk uninterrupted? Does he make you laugh?

Whatever it is, today as you walk, tell him why you like him, not just why you love him.

Day 23: Do It Again

Status check: Pick one thing you have done during this Challenge that has had the biggest impact on your husband. Do it again.

Write in your personal journal why you think it is so impactful.

Day 24: Pray for Him

Pray for your husband, then text or e-mail him about it. ("I know you have that big meeting with your boss, and I prayed _____ for you.")

Some men are demonstrative in prayer; others aren't. Yet regardless, nearly every man will like to know that someone is praying for him. It also demonstrates to your man that you are attentive to his day and what is going on in his life even when he's far away.

Day 25: Appreciate the Romance

Acknowledge the romantic efforts of your man and learn to see what he views as romantic. Not all men are comfortable being overtly charming in public, but it turns out that most men (85 percent) feel this way inside! They are secret romantics at heart; it's just that they also view going out and doing things together with their wives as romantic! When he wants to play golf together, do a hobby together, or even sit and watch the football game on TV together, notice that he wants to do that stuff *together,* and that is romantic to him. He just wants to be with you.

So what signs do you see that your husband wants to be with you? Is there anything your husband does to keep the romance in your relationship? Tell him today what you recognize and what it means to you. It will give him greater confidence in his romantic efforts.

And if you're creating a gift journal, be sure to note this there as well!

Day 26: Acknowledge Unseen Efforts

Think about the mundane things your husband does to keep the household going: earns money, takes out the trash, keeps up with the maintenance of your cars, maintains the lawn. Acknowledge the time those "unseen" efforts take and how grateful you are to have such a magnificent husband.

Notice his reaction; it may be the best incentive to say those things again, even after the Challenge is over! Of course, you do the menial and mundane too. But the 30-Day Kindness Challenge is about building great habits for a great relationship, and one vital habit is being mindful of the positive things about _your spouse._ So keep it up! You are just a few days from the end of the Challenge.

Day 27: Stay in the Moment

Today, in the _very_ next interaction you have with your husband, what is the kindest thing you could do for him? When he calls to tell you he'll be late for dinner, is it to speak in a more polite or kind tone of voice instead of a frustrated one? When he texts you to tell you he'll pick up Johnny on the way home instead of you having to do it, do you tell him, "You're such a great dad"? When he comes in from the day exhausted, would the kindest thing be to simply give him a hug and let him vanish to his man cave without pressure to talk?

Whatever your next interaction, think, _What is the kindest thing I can do right now?_ And do it.

Day 28: Believe He Wants to Make You Happy

Today, whether there's a conflict or it's a great day, assume the best of your spouse. Assume that he wants, above all, to make you happy. In our surveys nearly all spouses said they deeply cared about their mates. Yet among couples in so-so or struggling marriages, only about half of their mates said they believed that their spouses really did care about them! Sometimes without realizing it, we question whether our husbands really care.

Today, tell your husband that you know he wants to make you happy and that you see his efforts when he does _____. Thank him for it!

Day 29: **Write It Down**

Tomorrow is the last day of the Challenge, and for nearly a month you've been practicing the habit of catching negative words and thoughts and replacing them with positive ones.

So today, think about all those positive things you have noticed about your husband in the last month that might have slipped your day-to-day notice before. Create a "Top Five Things I Newly Appreciate About My Husband" list.

Make two copies, one for your personal journal and one, if appropriate, for your gift journal.

Note: If you're making a gift journal, think about how you want to give it to your husband. Do you want to wrap it and give it to him tomorrow? Or will you save it for a later date?

Important: If you two are doing the Challenge together, keep in mind that he may or may not have created a journal for you, and *that is okay.* The key is about building habits, which is what matters most!

Reminder: Once the Challenge is over, don't forget to take the assessment online at JoinTheKindnessChallenge.com again and see how you've improved!

Day 30: **You Did It!**

Congrats! You've reached the last day of the 30-Day Kindness Challenge!

Today, consider this question: What habit in word, thought, or action have you built that *your husband* would most want you to keep using? Restraining from criticism? Saying "thank you" for the things that he does? Doing a particular little act of kindness?

Would that habit likely have a great impact on the ongoing happiness of your marriage? If so, resolve to keep going with it!

Then, in your personal journal, write what most affected you and your husband about the 30-Day Kindness Challenge and what you most want to continue as a personal habit going forward. And if you want more ideas for the days ahead, consider reading *For Women Only,* a book about men, or *The Surprising Secrets of Highly Happy Marriages* about the simple habits that make great marriages. (You might also want to do a go-forward assessment at JoinTheKindnessChallenge.com. The key is to pick specific things to do to keep growing and challenging yourself toward kindness.)

Thanks for taking this thirty-day journey—
and *enjoy* the journey ahead!

Doing the Challenge for Your Wife

Men, thanks for doing the 30-Day Kindness Challenge. Note: Your Challenge is tailored with the husband's version of Element #1 (see chapter 9) rather than the general Element #1 to Nix the Negatives (see chapter 6). If you prefer to do the usual Element #1, though, have at it!

So here you go. For the next thirty days:

1. Don't be distracted and don't withdraw. Give your wife your full attention in conversation for at least fifteen minutes a day. (And when you are upset with each other, stay in the game five minutes past when you want to escape.)
2. Each day find at least one thing you enjoy or appreciate about her and tell her, and tell someone else.
3. Each day do one little act of kindness for her.

Day 1: The Challenge Begins Today!

And weeee're off! Today, soon after you and your wife are home after work hours, eliminate all distractions for fifteen minutes (physically put down your phone, turn off the TV) and ask her something specific about her day, something that can't be answered with "fine." ("What happened with your big presentation at work?" "Did the kids treat each other any better today?") Listen and ask follow-up questions.

Coach's Corner: Practice this type of listening well. It is a key habit you'll be building during the next thirty days—and something that will make her very, very happy.

Reminder: Don't forget to go to JoinTheKindnessChallenge.com to take the assessment before you get further into the Challenge. You can also sign up there to receive these types of tips via daily e-mail reminders instead.

Day 2: *What Is Your Wife Doing Today?*

What is your wife doing today? Same old same old, or something different? Whatever it is, text or call her *during the day* and ask her specifically how such and such went today.

Why does this matter? Seventy-five percent of all women on the survey said it deeply pleases them when their man texts or even leaves a voice mail during the day to say they are thinking about them. Showing that you are thinking about her even at work is code for "I love you."

Coach's Corner: Tonight, or whenever you have your fifteen minutes of full-attention listening, follow up on what she told you today. If your wife tends to be talkative and you're worried about being able to listen well if it goes beyond the time limit, perhaps preface the question with, "I've got to get Brandon to bed in about fifteen minutes, but before I do, I want to hear what happened with _____."

Day 3: *"I Do" Isn't the End of the Story*

Pick one of these statements to tell your wife tonight (and follow up in action if appropriate):

1. "I thought about you today."
2. "Let me watch the kids tonight. You deserve a break."
3. "Can I pray for you about that?"
4. "I'm turning off my phone and computer for the night."

Coach's Corner: Why do those phrases matter so much? To your wife, your "I do" probably wasn't the end of the story. Every day, most women subconsciously wonder, *"Do you" . . . still?*, especially after an argument, when she recognizes that she no longer looks like the bikini babe you married, or when her inner Cruella de Vil comes out. So every day she needs reassurance that you love her. The four statements above are examples of how to say exactly that. And developing a habit of signaling your continued interest will increase her security that, yes, you really do love her! (Which is why you'll find these ideas sprinkled through the coming days as well.)

You can read more about the power of these four phrases online at www.crosswalk.com/family/marriage/relationships/4-phrases-every-man-should-tell-his-wife-no-questions-asked.html.

Day 4: How to Bring a Smile to Her Face

What is one household chore that your wife does regularly that you'd hate to have to do? Either in person or written in a text or note, thank your wife for doing it all the time so you don't have to.

Also, if you decided to make a gift journal and haven't yet started it, start today. Each day write something different that you love, appreciate, or enjoy about your wife (such as doing this chore!), then give her the journal later as a present (for example, during a date night). It will be a spectacular gift that she will treasure.

Coach's Corner: You don't have to use the specific words "Thank you for doing the laundry" to express gratitude. It will bring a smile to her face even if you say something in guy-speak. ("If it weren't for you, honey, I'd be going commando every day. You're amazing.")

Day 5: She Worries: Listen and Offer to Pray

As verbal processors, most women tend to think things through by talking them through. Which means a husband will hear a lot of her worry thoughts. There is bound to be something she mentions today, or has mentioned recently, that you can ask her about during your fifteen-minute conversation/listening time.

When she brings up that worry, listen for a few minutes, ask how she's feeling about it so she gets a chance to talk it through, and then ask her if you can pray with or for her about that situation. (If you aren't comfortable praying together out loud, tell her you will pray for her today, and then tell her that you did.)

Coach's Corner: Has she mentioned something you've done so far in the Challenge? Even if she hasn't, persevere! She may simply be too busy to notice, or if your relationship is a bit rocky, she could be too withdrawn to engage right now. Even though kudos would be nice, these thirty days aren't about recognition. They are about changing your marriage, not just by using loving actions like learning how to listen, but by changing your own attitude, contentment, and happiness with your wife by focusing on the positives. The rewards will be worth it.

Day 6: *The Key to Really Pleasing Her*

What about sex? On Shaunti.com search for the article "Men, If You Want More Sex, Give Her Better Anticipation Time," which describes how to overcome a physiological difference between men and women that commonly gets in the way. Today or tomorrow, practice giving fun "anticipation time" cues and see what happens. You may need to ask her (during your talk time today?) how much anticipation time she needs. Some women need an entire day, others just a few hours, and a smaller percentage don't need anticipation time at all.

Christian sex therapists Debra Taylor and Michael Sytsma explain it this way:

> This [sexual desire] is a key area of misunderstanding be-
> tween husbands and wives. Many women have commented

to us, "I enjoy sex once we're 10 to 15 minutes into foreplay, and I think, Wow! We should do this more often! But during the week I hardly ever think about it. I wish I felt more sexual than I do, because I enjoy the closeness it brings."[1]

You can also read more at http://intimatemarriage.org/resources/73 -7-things-you-need-to-know-about-sex.html#sthash.4dhUHaJn.dpuf.

Coach's Corner: Have you wondered where sex fits into the Challenge? We're specifically *not* tying the two together because in most marriages (although not all), men already think about sex more than women, and many do caring things with sex in mind. But this unintentionally sabotages their efforts because it trains women to think, *He doesn't really care; he just wants to get lucky later.*

So during this thirty days, hug her just to hug her and be kind just to be kind. This does not mean abstaining from sex, but be aware about putting some time and space between your acts of kindness (or hugs) and your initiation of sex.

Day 7: Fight Fair

Accountability check: Reflect on how you've handled conflict and withdrawal during the Challenge and talk to your wife about it.

If you've had a conflict, did you stay in there five more minutes past when you wanted to escape (assuming you were in control of your temper and didn't need to escape to avoid saying or doing something hurtful)? If so, congratulations! Make note of *how* you did it.

Or did you say "Fine, have it your way!" as you walked out of the room? If so:

1. What could you do to help remain engaged?
2. Next time, before you walk out of the room, reassure her, "We'll figure this out, but I need a break to calm myself down right now."

Coach's Corner: In most cases, avoiding the temptation to escape is a good habit because it assures your wife right when she's at her most vulnerable. So ask your wife if hanging in there for an extra few minutes would mean something to her, and discuss how to do that. You'll be more likely to do it if you've already planned for it.

Then once you try it, make note of how it worked. The best way to build a good habit is not only to come up with success strategies for how to fix something that's going wrong but also to recognize when you've done it right. If you are keeping a personal journal, write down what you've learned on this subject. Or take one of our assessments at JoinTheKindnessChallenge.com to see what you're doing well and what you still need to work on.

Day 8: Get the Kids Involved

If you have children/stepchildren at home, do something today to help them appreciate your wife more. For example, pick one or more of these ideas:

- If they don't already, remind them to thank Mom when she serves a meal.
- Ask them what they did to help their mom/stepmom today. If they look at you blankly, ask them to take five minutes to come up with an idea and implement it at some point today or tomorrow. Then check to make sure they followed through.
- Train them on a household chore they can sometimes do for your wife.
- If you're creating a gift journal, have your kids write an appreciative note to your wife.

If your children are grown and gone, ask one or more to reach out with a phone call or e-mail to your wife just to say, "Thanks for being a great mom."

Coach's Corner: Mothers want to be appreciated on more than just Mother's Day. Developing a daily attitude of gratitude in your children is not only great for your wife, but it will help your kids learn that attitude in other areas of life as well.

Day 9: *It's the Thought That Counts*

Bring her a small gift today and say, "I was thinking of you." It could be her favorite candy, gum, a cute mug from the coffee shop where you had a meeting, or a pretty pen (women love the stationery aisle at Target, Walmart, or the bookstore).

Coach's Corner: Even though a woman's "love language" may not be giving and receiving gifts, it truly is the thought that counts. Even if you simply hand her the little three-ounce bottle of hazelnut syrup and say, "I saw this display when I was meeting Bill, and I know how much you like this stuff in your coffee," it tells her something priceless: *You were on my mind.*

Day 10: *Little Actions Have Big Impact*

Today, or the next time you're out together, as you walk through a parking lot somewhere or just sit reading or watching TV on the sofa, reach out and hold her hand. Or put your hand on her knee. Or put your arm around her.

These little actions signal to her that you would choose her all over again, which is one of the things she most needs to know day to day. And if you do this in public, that's a bonus in the value scale to her.

Tip: Don't try to initiate sex afterward. That way she won't feel that you are showing affection just because you want sex.

Coach's Corner: Sometimes we miss the little things that make the biggest impact on our spouses simply because they wouldn't impact us.

Watch your wife's reaction when you put your arm around her—it will probably make you want to do it again! Eighty-two percent of all women on our surveys said they were deeply pleased when their man reached out and took their hand. This is what we call high leverage: a little action with a big impact. Who knew?

Day 11: Affirm Her Every Day

How are you doing at finding something positive to praise in your wife each day? If you are struggling in your marriage or feel she doesn't appreciate you, it might be difficult to avoid focusing on the negatives.

Look for and make a list of real and positive things you appreciate about your wife. Write them in your personal journal and pick one as your affirmation for today (then you can refer back to the list on other days).

Coach's Corner: Whatever you focus on will grow. Train yourself to focus on the very real positives, including how she feels about you. Even among the most struggling couples on our surveys, 97 percent said they cared about their mates. In other words, your spouse almost certainly cares about you. Keep that firmly in mind as you train yourself to focus on the positive.

If your wife tends to be critical, it is easy to think, *I can't do anything right with her.* But try to stop yourself. Instead, tell yourself what is probably the truth—she doesn't realize how painful, irritating, belittling, or frustrating her criticism is for you—and look for all the ways she *does* appreciate you.

Day 12: Short but Sweet

Kindness idea: Where can you leave a short but sweet note of affection for your wife? On the mirror in the bathroom? The steering wheel of her car? Inside her purse? Maybe make a duplicate sticky note and put it in the journal if you are giving her one (that can be your journal entry for today).

Coach's Corner: "Have a good day" is not quite enough affection; you say the same to your UPS delivery guy. "Love you" is good, but see if you can also find other words that she'll hear as affection. For example: "I'm so glad I'm married to you." "Hi, beautiful." "You're the best person I know! I love you." "I can't imagine life without you."

Day 13: "Let Me Do That"

When your wife starts to do a household task tonight, step in. Without making a big deal of it, say, "Let me do that."

If you have children, consider asking them to help as part of teaching them how to honor their mom/stepmom. This teaches your kids how to serve others *in their home,* which is where servanthood should begin.

Coach's Corner: Out of the corner of your eye, observe your wife's reaction to your unexpected helpful action. If she's happy but matter-of-fact, that probably signals that she already sees you as someone who does this kind of thing, which is great. If she acts really surprised, or even suspicious, that signals that perhaps you need to do this a bit more often, which will be a great opportunity to be a hero to your wife.

Day 14: Meeting Her Needs May Be Simpler Than You Think

Is there something your wife has been saying that signals a particular need or wish? She may need something from you ("I wish you would call when you'll be late for dinner") or could just be dreaming out loud ("Wouldn't it be nice to take the kids to visit Yosemite someday?").

Whatever it is, bring it up and discuss it. Be willing to try to make a change if it would mean something to her.

Coach's Corner: Here's a tip about women: even if you don't see how you can meet a particular need ("But I can't always call when I'll be late since I am in client meetings!"), it will mean the world to her if you care enough to bring it up to brainstorm a solution rather than making her either nag you or drop it. And you might uncover creative possibilities you didn't consider before. (For example, surreptitiously texting "6/7+" under the table in the client meeting means "I said 6:00 p.m., but it is going to be after 7:00 before I leave.")

Day 15: *Midpoint Check: Look Both Inward and Outward*

Grab your personal journal, reflect on these two questions, and make notes about what you've learned.

First, look inward: Are you seeing any difference in yourself or how you feel about your marriage as a result of this Challenge? For example, is it easier to give that fifteen minutes of undistracted attention to your wife every day? Is it easier today than it was on Day 1 to think about her positive qualities or to plan ahead to do an act of kindness? If it is, you are making progress!

Second, look outward at your wife's cues: Are you seeing any differences in her or how she feels about you and your marriage? For example, how is she enjoying the daily fifteen minutes of undistracted attention from you? Is she more responsive to the acts of kindness or the words of love?

Coach's Corner: In our research, we've seen that one of the best things a man can do to make his marriage great is to become a student of his wife. To "learn" her. Not just her likes, dislikes, and favorite foods but how to read her. What does she respond to best? What are her signals of feeling flat? Hurt? Inspired? Loved? Learning her is worth all your time and effort. Once you read and follow the signals, you'll see the good ones come up a lot more often. (Consider taking one of the assessments at JoinTheKindnessChallenge.com to get specific action steps to work on.)

Day 16: *Tell Her She Is Beautiful*

At some point today or tomorrow morning, give your wife a big hug and tell her she's beautiful. Tell her specifically what is lovely about her. In my research 75 percent of all women surveyed said it "deeply pleases" them when they're sincerely told they're beautiful. This is one of the Fantastic Five little actions that the surveys indicate matter a lot to almost every woman. (The others are outlined in *The Surprising Secrets of Highly Happy Marriages.*)

Coach's Corner: Every woman wants to feel beautiful to her man, but some have given up hope. Your woman may not be tending to her outward appearance as much as she did when you first met, but she wants to be attractive to you. What about her feminine beauty charms you?

Day 17: *Fresh Air and Great Conversation*

Get some fresh air with your wife and take a walk around your neighborhood. Holding her hand at times will send a clear "I love you" signal. If the timing is better, defer to the weekend and take a hike together.

Coach's Corner: This can be your fifteen minutes of undivided attention if you talk about something close to her heart as you walk, rather than just about your favorite fantasy football team.

If you are making the gift journal and really want to score a home run, you could pick a leaf or flower, press it into the journal, date it, and add a sweet comment.

No, that would actually be a grand slam!

Day 18: Be Specific!

Send your wife a text telling her one *specific* thing you love and enjoy about her. Do it now, before you forget! (And add it to your journal too.) On the surveys, 75 percent of all women said messaging them during the day really pleased them.

Coach's Corner: If you are in a funk and feeling discontent about her today, for whatever reason, you don't have to feel that feeling of love right now. Just think back to the last time something you love about her came to mind. Text her about that.

A 2014 *Atlantic* article on John Gottman's research pointed out, "People who are focused on criticizing their partners miss a whopping 50 percent of positive things their partners are doing and they see negativity when it's not there."[2] Read more about the power of regularly practicing kindness toward your mate at www.theatlantic.com/health /archive/2014/06/happily-ever-after/372573.

Day 19: What Does She Think?

Has your wife noticed or said anything about your efforts in the 30-Day Kindness Challenge?

If so, let her know how it makes you feel when she acknowledges your efforts (even if she doesn't know about the Challenge itself). She simply may not realize how much it means to you when she says, "Thank you." A little nudge can help encourage her to encourage you.

If not, think through what is working well, what you might want to do differently, and what she is most responsive to, and try more of what she does respond to.

Coach's Corner: If she hasn't noticed your efforts or seems unmoved by them, consider whether something else needs to happen first. For example, if you have hurt her and that wound hasn't had closure, no amount of kindness or attentiveness will substitute for an apology. Once you apologize, she may be more open.

Day 20: Tell a Story

Recall something your wife did in the last few years that you really loved. Bring that story up and retell it so she knows how you felt about it. ("Do you remember that time we helped Frank and Jeannie when they got in that car accident? You were amazing.") Yes, this can count as your fifteen-minute full-attention time if you draw her into the conversation and listen to her.

Coach's Corner: Need a memory jogger about a story that might count? Think of some unique event, a special acknowledgment of an accomplishment, or how she complimented you in front of your friends, initiated a really awesome intimate time, or made a big effort to stick to the budget when times were tough. If you're creating the gift journal, immortalize the story and how she made you feel.

Day 21: Give Her a Break

Today tell her, "You deserve a break today. Let me watch the kids tonight." If you don't have kids at home who need to be watched, do something out of the ordinary for her just because she's extraordinary to you: fix dinner or bring home a special meal.

Coach's Corner: "Just because" moments are powerful. And they have even greater impact when they are unexpected. A "just because" message says "I love you" through *action*.

Day 22: Something Special

Today, reinforce one thing your wife does that makes you feel special. Tell her what she does and how it makes you feel. Thank her for it.

Your wife probably already tries to show you how important you are to her, and this lets her know that her efforts are noticed and meaningful to you. She will be more likely to repeat something if she knows it's working, especially if she wonders if you even notice.

Note: If the "something special" is related to sex, be careful to refrain from initiating sex right after you tell her this! That will build her trust in your intentions.

Coach's Corner: Are you having trouble thinking of something she does that makes you feel special? Think about your birthday or Father's Day and how those days are different because of your wife. How does she make those days stand out from the rest for you?

Or how does she treat you differently than she does the rest of the male population?

You don't have to find something big to mention. Anything she does that makes you feel special is worth noticing.

Day 23: The Beauty of Marriage

Think about your first dating days with your wife. What attracted you to her then *that you still see in her today*? Tell her about it, even if it is a text: "I was just thinking about the first time I saw you. Remember that restaurant? I thought you were the most beautiful girl I'd ever seen. Still do." If you can, bring up the whole story and reminisce about it.

If you're making a gift journal, the story would be a great one to recount.

Coach's Corner: The beauty of dating is that everything about your partner is fresh and new. The beauty of marriage is that you can be honest and vulnerable and *tell* each other what you were thinking during those early days, in a way you never would have dared at the time! So use that ability to be more open!

Day 24: Those Unseen Efforts

Think about the mundane things your wife does to keep the household going: pay the bills, manage the health insurance, track the stacks of school paperwork, or stay on top of the kids' dentist visits and your sister's birthday. Today, acknowledge the time those unseen efforts take and how grateful you are to have such a magnificent wife.

Coach's Corner: Notice her reaction; it may be the best incentive for a repeat performance! Of course, you do the menial and mundane too. But the Kindness Challenge is about building great habits for a great relationship, and one vital habit is being mindful of the positive things about her. So keep it up! You are just six days from the end of the Challenge.

Day 25: Break Out of the Shackles of Routine

Spontaneity test! Today or tonight, do something completely spontaneous that she will enjoy. Tell her, "I'm turning off my phone, computer, or TV for the night," and just hang around and talk as you do chores together. Or take her out for a cup of coffee during her work break or a doughnut after dinner, or even suggest a last-minute "Hey, I know it is a school night, but the kids don't have homework. Let's go to a movie!" What can you do that would be fun and spontaneous?

Coach's Corner: It may feel artificial, but every now and then, doing something spontaneous just for the fun of it is a great way to show you care. Why? Because it shows that you're actually willing to pull yourself out of your routine to do something fun for the two of you. If you like spontaneity but think your wife won't (or can't because of school obligations for the kids), start today to drop a hint that in a day or two you want to do something crazy, just for fun, to let her get used to the idea.

Day 26: Brew Up Some Love

Just five days left! Today, bring your wife her morning coffee or tea or whatever she drinks, just how she likes it.

Coach's Corner: Becoming an expert takes time, and you've been investing the time during this Challenge to be purposeful and learn what matters to your wife. Hopefully you see that taking the time to become an expert about your wife's preferences and desires—how she likes her coffee is just one of many examples!—pays great dividends.

Day 27: What Makes You Feel Great?

Did your wife say or do something recently that made you feel great? (For example, did she recently tell you that she liked how you handled homework with the kids?) She probably doesn't know that it even stood out to you, so tell her. (And if you're creating a gift journal, this would be a great story to retell.)

Coach's Corner: Whenever you want a repeat performance, positive feedback signals to her that you noticed and value what she did or said.

Day 28: Review and Repeat

Pick the one thing you have done during this Challenge that has had the biggest impact on your wife. Do it again.

Coach's Corner: In the research with thousands of men and women, it is clear that most spouses are trying hard to please each other. But they are often trying hard at the wrong things because they assume their spouse likes what they like. So watch what brings the greatest impact to your wife, do it again, and record in your personal journal why you think it was so impactful.

Day 29: *It's a Date!*

Pick a day on the calendar a week or two from now and set a date night with your wife. Even better, commit to taking a date night regularly. You've hopefully seen the benefit of regular time together with your wife during this Challenge, so plan for a way to keep that going!

Coach's Corner: Tomorrow is the last day of the Challenge! If you're making a gift journal, think about how you want to give it. Do you want to wrap the journal and give it to her tomorrow, or are you saving it for a later date? If you're saving it for later, keep it handy and even continue adding to it. You might find that the habit you've built is worth continuing—either in a gift journal or as standalone notes to her, which are a great way to say "I love you."

Reminder: Once the Challenge is over, don't forget to take the assessment online at JoinTheKindnessChallenge.com and see how you've improved!

Day 30: *Finish the Course Set Before You*

Congratulations! Today, give yourself kudos for finishing the course! Now consider: What habit would your wife most want you to keep using? Listening for fifteen minutes? Telling her the things you enjoy about her? Doing little acts of kindness? Which habit had the most impact on your happiness, your wife's happiness, or both? Pick what you want most to keep going and resolve to do so!

194 Thirty Days of Kindness Tips

Coach's Corner: Send yourself a text or e-mail every day or two with "next steps," which will make you more likely to do them. For example: "Give her the gift journal on our date night next Friday" or "Continue to listen for fifteen minutes a day." And consider reading *For Men Only* (our book about women) or *The Surprising Secrets of Highly Happy Marriages* (about the simple habits that make great marriages) for more tips going forward!

Thanks for taking this thirty-day journey—
and *enjoy* the journey ahead!

Doing the Challenge for Anyone

Pick a member of your personal, professional, or geographic community (your boss, romantic partner, child, neighbor, in-laws) as your target for kindness in the hopes of improving your relationship. This should be someone with whom you interact fairly regularly (whether in person or via phone or e-mail).

Note: Since every relationship is different, adapt the Challenge and the daily tips as necessary for the closeness of the relationship and how often you see each other. But in general, for thirty days:

1. Say nothing negative about your person, either to them or about them to somebody else. (If negative feedback is unavoidable—such as when you must correct the mistake of a child or colleague—be constructive, helpful, and encouraging and speak without a negative tone. For example, "Yes, the boss was in a bad mood today. The executive committee is probably on his case. Let's stay focused and deliver a great report.")

2. Every day (or as often as possible), find one thing positive that you can sincerely praise or affirm about your person and tell them, *and* tell someone else. (Tell your mother-in-law, "Thanks for being willing to watch the kids last night while we were at that meeting," then tell your husband the same thing—*without* bringing up that she let the kids stay up way too late again.)

3. Every day (or as often as possible), do one small act of kindness or generosity for your person.

Day 1: Communicate Kudos

Find something your person has done recently that is praiseworthy and compliment them on it. "You did a great job at that sales presentation last week." "Way to go to baseball practice even though you didn't feel like it." "Mom, I heard you got a big award—congrats!"

Day 2: Share the Load

Choose a task you know your person dislikes and do it with a cheerful attitude and no expectation. Take your neighbor's garbage can to the curb on trash pickup day; clean the dirty mugs in the office break room sink even though it is your colleague's day to do it; offer to drop the other soccer mom's son at home so she doesn't have to come back to the ball fields in traffic.

Day 3: Offer Understanding

Is your person a complainer you think is *wrong*? Today (or the next time this comes up), no matter how off base you might think they are, provide no corrective dialogue but simply say something understanding such as, "I bet that did make you frustrated" or "I'm sorry you have had a rough start to your day."

Day 4: Compliment the Questionable

What is one thing your person probably likes about themself but perhaps thinks you don't? (Their strong opinions, which you see as being uncompromising; their ability to go with the flow, which you see as never being on time; their interest in art, when you wish they would focus on math.) Today, compliment them *in the area they think you dislike.* ("I saw how you were so willing to stop what you were doing when Kayla needed to talk. I could learn from your flexibility.") Bonus points if you can do it in print (a note, an e-mail, and so on) that they can look back on just to be sure you did indeed say that!

Day 5: Share Snacks

Leave a snack of their choice (would that be a healthy food bar or a doughnut?) on the counter (at work, in the house) or wherever you know they will see it.

Day 6: Offer Encouragement

Everyone makes mistakes and is touched by unconditional support and encouragement, especially when they don't deserve it. The next time your person suffers consequences from a mistake (gets a bad grade on a test, is embarrassed in a meeting, mentions the criticism they got from their spouse), offer your unconditional support and encouragement with no mention of what they did wrong. (For example, if your child got a bad test grade, say, "I'm so sorry, honey. In the next week, do you want me to help you e-mail the teacher about any extra work you can do to give your grade a boost?")

Day 7: Accountability Check

How are you doing at saying nothing negative, either to your person or about them to somebody else? Look back on the past week and identify any cases where you *were* negative despite your efforts. In a journal or notebook, list them. Next to each, identify the reasons why you think you slipped up ("I'm so tempted to join in when my colleagues are dissing my boss because I want to fit in") and what you could have done differently to prevent the negativity from occurring ("I think I just need to leave the break room when they start talking about her"). Pick one or two success strategies to employ next time. Perhaps take one of the assessments at JoinTheKindnessChallenge.com to identify how you're doing and what you most need to work on.

Day 8: *Thank 'Em*

Find one thing your person has done recently that you can be thankful for and send them an e-mail, text, or note of thanks. ("I saw that you put away the DVDs in the living room the way I asked. Thanks for doing that." "Thanks for stepping up for me in that meeting yesterday." "I noticed that you asked Mom to back off a bit. I appreciate that." "You're awesome for always bringing snacks to the kids' volleyball games.")

Day 9: *Think Drink*

Make or bring your person a coffee or other favorite beverage, your treat. If you work in an office with them, buy them their favorite coffee drink on your way back from lunch. If you live with your person, make them that complicated smoothie they like so much.

Day 10: *Tackle Insecurity*

When your person looks in the mirror or contemplates their life, what do you think they worry about? That they will miss their sales targets and the team will be upset? That they aren't beautiful? That no one likes working with them? Say something today that will touch your person's heart and encourage them in that area. ("You've been working your tail off, and the team has noticed." "You've got the most beautiful hair, honey." "I really enjoyed doing this project with you.")

Day 11: *Be Thoughtful*

E-mail your person a news article or blog they would appreciate (about their favorite politician, sports team, or industry area of expertise) or text them a picture of something you know they really like (their favorite car, favorite movie or actor) with a note such as, "Thought you might enjoy this article" or "Thought about you when I ran across this today."

Day 12: Get Along

Today, don't argue with your person. Unless it is something life- or business-altering, defer to them instead. Politely and positively let them know that although you disagree, you're fine with doing it their way. ("Although my preference is to log the students' science fair projects this other way, I know you've thought this through, so let's give your way a try.")

Day 13: Brag on 'Em

Today, look for a way to praise your person in front of their boss, teacher, parent, or someone whose opinion really matters to them. ("Yeah, Ben's great at putting things together, isn't he? He's actually been building this outdoor fireplace in his backyard that is so cool all the neighbors keep coming over to look at it.") If you're not going to see your person today, put a reminder on your calendar for the next time you will see them.

Day 14: Accountability Check

How are you doing at finding something you can appreciate or praise about your person each and every day—and telling them and telling at least one other person? If you realize you could do better, write in your journal or notebook specifically what you've missed or where you've messed up, and why. Consider and implement a success strategy to address it. ("I see my high-school daughter every day, so I can remember to praise her. But I forget to say those positive things about her to someone else. I will post a sticky note on my computer each day to remind me to mention good things about her to friends or colleagues.")

Day 15: Return the Favor

In the past few weeks or months, what is one thing your person has said or done for you? What type of action was it? An act of service? A word of affirmation? A gift of some kind? An out-of-the-blue kind comment? Or perhaps simply not criticizing you when they might have otherwise? Whatever it was, it likely indicates that type of action would be meaningful for them. So do that same type of action for them today.

Day 16: Kill Conflict with Kindness

If your person is someone with whom you sometimes have conflict, plan ahead for a positive response. The next time (today or later) they say anything that ruffles your feathers, respond with a compliment or kind word. ("Yes, I know I probably didn't leave on time to get here. Thanks so much for watching the kids. You're always so willing, and it was my fault that I left work a bit late.")

Day 17: Let 'Em Laugh

E-mail or text your person a joke or funny video, something that is their type of humor, with a note. ("Oh man, this made me laugh. I thought you would get a kick out of it.")

Day 18: Share Sweet Memories

Recall a memory of something kind that your person did for you in the past and retell it to them today, with a particular focus on how it made or makes you feel (then or now). ("Honey, remember when you brought me that pillow you made in art class that took you a whole month to embroider? That was so sweet of you. It made me feel really special.")

Day 19: Jump In

Is your person working on a difficult project for work, volunteer activities, or school? Offer to help them and follow through without getting annoyed or exasperated. ("I'm so sorry the volunteers for the event have been so difficult to work with. How about I bring over some food and desserts tomorrow so you can butter them up?")

Day 20: Practice Prayer

Find something your person is especially worried or sad about and tell them you'll pray for them—and then tell them that you did. ("Boss, I'm so sorry your mom hasn't been getting better. I think you know I'm a person of faith, and I'll be praying for her.") Or if appropriate, such as with a family member or friend, pray for your person right there.

Day 21: Accountability Check

Of the three daily Challenge elements (say nothing negative, practice praise, do a small act of kindness), which one is easiest to do and which is the most difficult? Write down the reasons for both, as well as what you most want to keep doing because it's working well, and what you need to stop doing in order to build your relationship with your person. The assessments at JoinTheKindnessChallenge.com may help you identify these.

Day 22: Practice Positivity

If you catch yourself getting frustrated with your person, stop your train of thought and say something positive about them. Say it to them if they are around or to someone else if they aren't.

Day 23: Erase That

Have you spoken negatively about your person to someone else in the past? (For example, have you complained about your stepson to your colleagues?) Make a list of the main people you've complained to, and today (and over the next few weeks) casually bring up with them what you now appreciate about your person. ("Did I tell you that Alan's son got accepted to his first-choice college? He worked really hard this past year to bring his grades up.")

Day 24: Cheer 'Em On

What does your person have going on today? If you're physically in the same place (home, office), leave a sticky note of encouragement about it where they will see it. ("Praying for your big discussion today!") If you're physically separated, e-mail, text, or call them about it.

Day 25: Follow It Up

How did your person's plans go yesterday? Ask how it went, then further encourage them by saying, "Great job," "You are so good at that stuff," "I'm hoping that will turn out well in the end," or other praise wherever possible—or commiserations where appropriate.

Day 26: Thank 'Em Again

What can you say "thank you" for today? Be on the lookout and tell your person as soon as you see it. ("Thanks for allowing me extra time to work through that presentation." "Wow, sweetheart, thanks for packing your lunch so I didn't have to." "I saw how you spoke kindly even though he was driving you crazy. Thanks for always being careful about that.")

Day 27: Send Seasonal Treats

Give your person a box of Girl Scout Cookies, Boy Scout popcorn, or some other seasonal goodies.

Day 28: Repeat Again

We're getting near the end of our thirty days! Think back: What is the one thing your person has most positively responded to during this 30-Day Kindness Challenge? Pick that same type of thing and do it again.

Reminder: Once the Challenge is over, don't forget to take the assessment online at JoinTheKindnessChallenge.com to see how you've improved!

Day 29: Praise Publicly

Now that you've been focusing on the positives in your person for almost a month, what rises up in your mind as a great character trait, skill, or other distinctive quality worth celebrating? Consider how you can make others aware of that trait in a way that will be meaningful for your person, then do it. (Submit your colleague's name as a contender for "customer service rep of the month," tell your pastor that your stepdaughter would probably love to sing as part of the worship team if asked, submit your father-in-law's woodworking designs for a community award.)

Day 30: Keep It Going

You've made it! It's thirty days later and we hope you see how avoiding the negatives, practicing the positives, and doing small acts of generosity have not only changed your relationship with your person but also lightened your heart. Today, look back on all you've learned. Consider taking an assessment at JoinTheKindnessChallenge.com to identify what you're doing well and what you still need to work on. Then consider: What is the one thing you want to make sure you keep doing as you move forward? Make a commitment to do so and tell someone else for accountability. And enjoy what happens!

Thanks for taking this thirty-day journey—
and *enjoy* the journey ahead!

Acknowledgments

This book and the research study behind it represent the effort and investment of many hundreds of people. I wish I could properly thank everyone! I also wish I could take each of you to dinner, not just because it is one way to say thanks, but because it would be fun to hang out with you. You are a spectacular, generous group of human beings, and I have really enjoyed interacting with each of you.

Among the core group who poured themselves into this project, I most have to acknowledge and pledge my lifelong indentured servitude to the astoundingly talented people on my staff, especially Caroline Niziol, who managed the entire 30-Day Kindness Challenge test project from start to finish; and Deanna Hamilton, my outstanding research and survey analyst on this initiative; as well as Linda Crews, my staff and operations director who came up with the idea of widely offering the Challenge to begin with; Theresa Colquitt, my executive assistant; Tally Whitehead, senior researcher; Naomi Duncan, director of client development; Nola Meyer, who manages all partner relationships; Angela Bouma and Lucy Iloenyosi, our designers; Charlyn Elliott and Dixie Walker who help so much with our Challenge applications; and the other team members I depend on every day. You all are amazing, and I am so very grateful for you. If we ever get some giant windfall from an anonymous benefactor, you all deserve an extended vacation in Hawaii. Or somewhere very remote where no one is e-mailing, calling, or texting at all hours of the day. And night.

In addition, I am immensely thankful for the generous and very practical help of the many dozens of people who worked with us to create the 30-Day Kindness Challenge test and research groups, as well as the hundreds of people who participated in the research, tested the Challenge, provided feedback, and contributed their insights via lengthy interviews and focus groups. I'm particularly grateful for Scott and Sherry Jennings at The Bridge in North Carolina; Kim and Dave Anderson and Jeff Simmons at Men's Leadership Network in Nashville; Jo Anna Williams at Christian Worship Center in San Diego; and multiple current and former leaders and representatives of the national iDisciple organization, especially Amber Mette, Emily Fernie, Nicole McNair, Shaundra Welch, and many others. (Big thanks to Summer Pridemore for stepping in to manage all the social media/tests during Caroline's maternity leave!) Thanks also to Shennelle Edwards, Tyler Reagin, Rob Pace, and many other expert professionals in the fields of psychiatry, psychology, leadership, technology, and neuroscience, who provided specialized help and offered insight into what my surveys were finding along the way. Special appreciation goes to all my manuscript readers, including fellow ASPIRE tour speaker Kerri Pomarolli, who contributed her creativity, and especially Morgen Feldhahn, who contributed her insight, perspective, and a touch of eye-rolling to keep me from saying anything particularly silly.

I'm also grateful for several people without whom this book wouldn't exist. I would never have thought to start this particular research were it not for the wisdom of Nancy DeMoss Wolgemuth, who created and shared the Husband Encouragement Challenge. Without Dr. Chuck Cowan of Analytic Focus, I never would have been able to do this or any other research surveys. And the ongoing insight and intervention of my amazing agent, Calvin Edwards, has been a prerequisite for this and every other book project.

At WaterBrook I'm in awe of my wonderful editors, Susan Tjaden and Holly Halverson; publisher Alex Field; and the many dozens of people who labor behind the scenes to take the raw material of these studies and books and turn them into something that is beautiful and life changing. I appreciate our partnership more than I can say.

Speaking of partners, I am deeply indebted to Nancy French for a lifetime of friendship, creative ideas for this project, and long dinners at fun restaurants; and especially to John and Jean Kingston and the team at Six Seeds/Patheos for their tremendous sponsorship of the JoinTheKindnessChallenge.com website, excellently developed by Phil Earnest and Rhen Bovi. I'm so grateful to a generous community of author/speaker partners, especially Les and Leslie Parrott for their many hours of Glamour-worthy assessment advice, and Kathi Lipp and Dave Willis for supporting the vision from its earliest days. I'm indebted to the staff and leaders of all our 30-Day Kindness Challenge partner organizations, especially Greg Smalley, Danny Huerta, and the rest of the Focus on the Family team for their encouragement and partnership. I'm also thankful for the friendship and help of the leaders and pastors at Perimeter Church.

Finally, to my prayer team, close friends, and family: You all are a treasure to me. Without you, I'm quite sure I wouldn't be able to handle any of this crazy life, business, and ministry! Especially to Mom, Dad, my sweet kids, and my amazing husband, Jeff: You hold me up, cover my mistakes with love, and help turn any discouragement to delight. Thank you for always being there for me in the most practical, patient, and caring of ways. I'm grateful for how you model the type of unconditional kindness I would someday like to be able to display—the kindness of the One to whom I am most grateful of all.

Notes

The epigraph for this book and variations on it have also been attributed to Plato and the Scottish author Ian Maclaren.

Chapter 1: Kindness Makes the World Go Round

1 As just one example of how much kindness has slipped as a cultural priority, in books published in American English between 1829 and 2007 (the most recent year available), the prevalence of the word *kindness* dropped almost 80 percent. (Based on an Ngram search for "kindness" and "Kindness" using the default smoothing of 7; conducted on https://books.google.com, September 2015. In 1829 the percent was .0049325. In 2007 it had declined 79 percent to .0010251.)

2. Throughout this book, various interview and survey quotes have been edited for length and clarity, and names and identifying details have been changed.

3. Luke 6:27, 35.

Chapter 2: Kindness Is a Superpower

1. Unless otherwise noted, all survey comments are responses from one of the test or primary survey groups conducted throughout the course of 2015 and early 2016; some have been edited and/or (if from the same individual) combined for clarity.

2. "And if you do good to those who are good to you, what credit is that to you? Even 'sinners' do that" (Luke 6:33, NIV). See Luke 6:27–36.

3. Luke 6:31.

Chapter 3: Is Kindness Ever the Wrong Approach?

1. Romans 12:18, NIV.

2. Romans 2:4.

Chapter 4: Kindness in Practice

1. See Philippians 4:2–8.

2. It is important to note that although mirror neurons are very likely one element in empathy for others, they are definitely not the only one. In some ways, though, the name "mirror neurons" has become a bit of a (simplistic) catchall name for the whole neurological process of developing empathy. There are a host of studies addressing how mirror neurons work and what we know and don't know. For example, see http://rstb.royalsocietypublishing.org/content /369/1644/20130169, as well as this one: www.sciencedirect.com/science /article/pii/S0168010214002314.

3. Travelmail Reporter, "Shock horreur: Finance minister tells cash-strapped (and perennially rude) French to be NICE to tourists," *Daily Mail,* June 20, 2014, www.dailymail.co.uk/travel/article-2663673/France-told-nicer-visitors-boost-tourism.html; "Smile S'il Vous Plait, Paris Needs Tourists," *Sky News,* July 15, 2009.

4. "TripAdvisor Names 2013 Travelers' Choice Destinations," May 21, 2013, www.tripadvisor.com/PressCenter-i6010-c1-Press_Releases.html.

Chapter 6: Nix the Negatives

1. See details at www.prisonexp.org.

2. Michael B. Lewis, PhD, and Patrick J. Bowler, MB, BS, "Botulinum toxin cosmetic therapy correlates with a more positive mood," *Journal of Cosmetic Dermatology* 8 (2009): 24, http://onlinelibrary.wiley.com/doi/10.1111/j.1473 -2165.2009.00419.x/epdf.

3. Lewis and Bowler, "Botulinum," 26.

4. From an e-mail conversation with Lysa TerKeurst, March 28, 2016.

5. See Brad J. Bushman, "Does Venting Anger Feed or Extinguish the Flame?," March 20, 2001, www-personal.umich.edu/~bbushman/PSPB02.pdf, as well as his *Psychology Today* article, "Anger Management: What Works and What Doesn't," September 25, 2013, www.psychologytoday.com/blog/get-psyched /201309/anger-management-what-works-and-what-doesnt.

6. Dr. William James, *The William James Reader Vol. 1* (New York: Start Publishing, 2012), Kindle edition, emphasis added.

7. Telephone interview with the author, April 7, 2015.

8. "I have learned to be content whatever the circumstances. I know what it is to be in need, and I know what it is to have plenty. I have learned the secret of being content in any and every situation, whether well fed or hungry, whether living in plenty or in want. I can do everything through him who gives me strength" (Philippians 4:11–13, NIV).

9. *Oxford Dictionaries,* s.v. "bitter," accessed July 21, 2016, www.oxforddictionaries .com/us/definition/american_english/bitter.

10. Roger Kimball, "The Rise of the College Crybullies," *Wall Street Journal,* November 13, 2015, www.wsj.com/articles/the-rise-of-the-college-crybullies -1447458587.

11. 2 Timothy 2:23, NIV.

12. See 2 Timothy 2:23–26.

13. See the book of 2 Samuel for the story.

14. "When Jesus spoke again to the people, he said, 'I am the light of the world. Whoever follows me will never walk in darkness, but will have the light of life'" (John 8:12, NIV).

15. Luke 11:33–36, NIV 2011.

Chapter 8: Carry Out Kindness

1. For more about John Gottman's findings, see Emily Esfahani Smith, "Masters of Love," *The Atlantic,* June 12, 2014, www.theatlantic.com /health/archive/2014/06/happily-ever-after/372573. For more about Brad Wilcox's findings, see the National Marriage Project, "When Baby Makes Three," *The State of Our Unions,* 2011, www.stateofourunions.org/2011 /when-baby-makes-three.php, especially the survey on marital generosity. For more about my own findings, see *The Surprising Secrets of Highly Happy Marriages* (Colorado Springs: Multnomah, 2013).

2. 2 Timothy 2:24.

3. *Looking for America* was presented as a series of ABC specials in 1996 and 1997. The quote from Jay Schadler is from memory, as many attempts to find the video or transcript have been unsuccessful. Jay Schadler's ABC biography can be seen at http://abcnews.go.com/Primetime/story?id=583107.

4. Psalm 18:35, NASB.

5. The National Marriage Project, "When Baby Makes Three," *The State of Our Unions,* 2011, www.stateofourunions.org/2011/when-baby-makes-three.php. Among wives with above average sexual satisfaction, 45 percent said they were "very happy" in marriage, compared to just 6 percent with below average sexual satisfaction who said they were very happy. For men, it was 45 percent compared to 7 percent. As Dr. Wilcox said, "Sexually satisfied wives enjoy a 39-percentage-point premium in the odds of being very happy in their marriages, and . . . sexually satisfied husbands enjoy a 38-percentage-point premium in marital happiness."

6. See my article on this phenomenon at www.patheos.com/blogs/askshaunti /2015/05/should-i-pray-for-god-to-make-me-more-um-amorous. One journal article on sexual stimulation (or lack thereof) resulting in higher or lower libido can be found at www.nature.com/ijir/journal/v14/n2/full/3900832a.html.

Thirty Days of Kindness Tips: Men Doing the Challenge for Their Wives

1. Debra Taylor and Michael Sytsma, "7 Things You Need to Know About Sex," Building Intimate Marriages, http://intimatemarriage.org/resources/73-7 -things-you-need-to-know-about-sex.html#sthash.4dhUHaJn.dpuf.
2. Emily Esfahani Smith, "Masters of Love," *The Atlantic,* June 12, 2014, www .theatlantic.com/health/archive/2014/06/happily-ever-after/372573.